W9-AVC-637

Renoir *Paris and the Belle Epoque*

Karin Sagner-Düchting

Renoir

*Paris and
the Belle Epoque*

Prestel

Munich · New York

Contents

7 La Grenouillère – New Shores in Sight

25 Paris in the Belle Epoque

41 Paradise on Earth in Montmartre

63 "He has painted the woman of Paris"

81 "A perpetual holiday and a mix of all classes"

93 Days under the Trees at the River

101 Dancing Couples – Images of Vitality and Joy

111 Biographical Notes

122 Notes

124 Selected Bibliography

125 List of Illustrations

La Grenouillère – New Shores in Sight

Visitors to the pleasure grounds and bathing pools at La Grenouillère used to walk across the Bougival Bridge – as painted by
Claude Monet in 1870. Or if they were coming from Chatou, only
twenty minutes by train from the Paris station Saint-Lazare – they
could cover the last mile or so to the river on foot or by coach. Besides holiday-makers who would take inexpensive lodgings in the
surrounding area and cross over to La Grenouillère on ferries,
these visitors were mainly Parisians making day trips at weekends
and on public holidays. Initially favoured by the upper classes, it
was in the 1860s that La Grenouillère became widely popular.
Renoir later described how he had come to know it through Prince
Georges Bibesco,[1] who commissioned designs from him for decoration work on his palace from 1868 onwards. While the secluded
coves of La Grenouillère were a favourite haunt above all for court-
ing couples, the place had just as much to offer for water-sports
enthusiasts – particularly swimmers and rowers.

The name La Grenouillère, meaning "frog-pond," has nothing to
do with the local fauna – for "frogs" was in fact what men called
those women of easy virtue who spent the summer months there.
These "frogs," "footloose girls who typified the Parisian standards
of the day... and who played an important role during the years
before and after the fall of the Empire," were "good sorts" as far as
Renoir was concerned, because they would pose for him.[2] A visit
by Napoleon III and his wife Eugénie in the summer of 1869 added
to the fame of the La Grenouillère. Contemporary illustrations
(page 9) aroused interest in La Grenouillère as an oasis for world-
weary city-dwellers; they may have also influenced Monet and Renoir.[3] Perhaps Renoir also felt that choosing to paint a well-known
subject in that year might increase the chances of his work being
accepted by the Salon, which until then had only exhibited his
works in 1864 and 1865.

La Grenouillère,
1869, detail

7

In August and September 1869, Renoir stayed nearby at his parents' house in Voisin by Louveciennes[4] while Monet had rooms in Bougival, from where he wrote to Bazille in September describing the plans he and Renoir had for a painting of La Grenouillère: "I have a dream, a picture, the bathers at La Grenouillère. I have done some poor sketches for it, but it is only a dream. Renoir, who has just spent two months here, also wants to paint this motif."[5] In 1868 Raoul de Presles writing in the journal *l'Evénement Illustré*

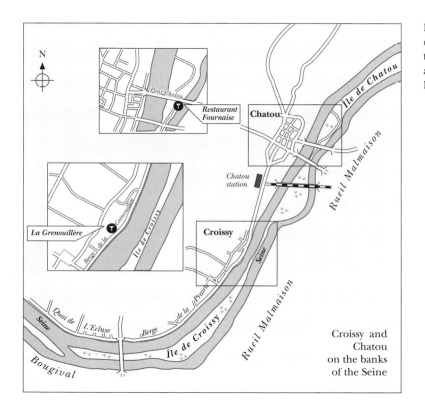

Favoured by Parisian
day-trippers:
the Restaurant Fournaise
and the Island
La Grenouillère

Croissy and
Chatou
on the banks
of the Seine

described how La Grenouillère looked in those days: "La Grenouillère is the Trouville of the Seine, a meeting place for those noisy, coquettish Parisians who spend the summer in Croissy, Chatou and Bougival. ... A green and white painted wooden structure with a platform in front of it had been put up on a firmly anchored barge. ... Refreshments were served in a large room that was

Top:
Jules Pelocq
La Grenouillère, 1868

Right:
Advertisement for the Island
Bal de la Grenouillère

Bottom:
Edouard Riou
La Grenouillère à Bougival, 1869

open to one side. ... To the right there were changing rooms, boat-houses and other outbuildings."[6]

Up until now, and even recently, writers on Renoir have referred to La Grenouillère as being on one of the islands in the Seine, l'Ile de Croissy. Careful reading of Guy de Maupassant's descriptions and an examination of contemporary illustrations, however, show that it was situated on the steep right bank of the Seine in Croissy (Berge de la Grenouillère) in the so-called "dead" arm of the Seine. La Grenouillère was linked to l'Ile de Croissy opposite it by a wooden walkway and a much-used ferry.

The floating building bearing the sign "Location des Canotiers" (Boats for Hire) was accessible via a small round island and some very simple, but nonetheless picturesque wooden walkways. The island, which measured less than twelve square meters, and which had one wonderfully decorative willow tree at its centre, was known for its shape as the "Camembert" and the crowd loved to squeeze onto it. On the left, there was a small fenced-off bathing area. Dozens of rowing-boats were moored by it since rowers were particularly welcome at the "Location des Canotiers" area. A few years later, in his short story *La Femme de*

Ferdinand Heilbuth
La Grenouillère, 1870

10

Bridge Near Paris, 1875

Overleaf: *La Grenouillère*, 1869 (Winterthur version)

Paul, Guy de Maupassant described La Grenouillère in very different terms. In his eyes it was a noisy meeting-place for the rabble. Renoir repeatedly took Maupassant to task for his pessimism, while the latter retaliated with talk of Renoir's rose-tinted spectacles.

Whatever the case, La Grenouillère was clearly a great attraction at that time. It was not only the theme of works by several contemporary illustrators (page 10),[7] but was also the subject of an oil-painting by Ferdinand Heilbuth that was shown in the Salon in 1870.

Unlike other contemporary illustrations of La Grenouillère, which were often specifically intended for publicity purposes, Renoir and Monet both painted on site in oils.

Four versions of La Grenouillère by Renoir are known. The version in Moscow and a privately owned version show the banks of the river, with the Seine on the right and people walking along the shore on the left. The version in Wintherthur (pages 12 / 13) has at its centre the narrow wooden walkway that links the artificial island with the river bank and the restaurant. Sweeping even further round to the right, the Stockholm Museum version (page 15) focuses on the small round island.

Claude Monet (page 16) painted the same subject from almost exactly the same position as Renoir chose for his Stockholm painting, making it possible to compare his work and Renoir's and clearly showing the basic differences between the two artists. Monet's concern was evidently to show the shimmering of the water's surface, the play of light and shade. His composition seems at once both more thought-out and bolder than Renoir's. The round stage-like form of the island is echoed in the concentric arrangement of the boats in the foreground and balanced by the diagonals of the walkways and the floating restaurant. In this way, the viewer's attention is directed towards the surface of the water, which is Monet's real theme in this work. And so it seems that the bathers, the people in the restaurant, and the figures on the artificial island are no more than stage props. Strong, coarse brushstrokes in blue-green, white, yellow, and black[8] along with stark contrasts of light and dark tones, create the impression of light-reflections on the moving surface of the water.

In Renoir's version, on the other hand, the brushstrokes, the colouration (light yellow-green), and the details, all go to create a warmer effect. More differentiated colours allow for gentler transitions from one brushstroke to the next. The contrasts are milder than Monet's, whose somewhat detached approach is focused entirely on technical and painterly matters, whereas Renoir has human concerns closer to heart. Renoir's composition is clear and calm in its structure (due to the predominance of horizontals and verticals) and also has as its motif the crowded little island, which was sometimes affectionately nicknamed the "flowerpot" because of the green latticework construction of its wooden floor.

This work is notable for its detailed figures, where considerable care has been taken to show the fashions of the day. Renoir's interest is in their outward appearance, in the fascination of the very materials themselves. Fashion-conscious young ladies take the air in summer dresses featuring the bustles[9] that came into fashion in 1868. The lady on the right, with her plate-hat set at a jaunty angle across her forehead, has her curls bunched up high, with some falling down onto the nape of her neck. It is impossible

La Grenouillère, 1869
(Moscow version)

Claude Monet, *La Grenouillère*, 1869

La Grenouillère, 1869

not to see the similarities with Renoir's *Lise* of 1867 (page 21), which he successfully exhibited in the Salon one year later. Renoir had met Lise Tréhot in 1865. She became his mistress and was his favourite model until 1872.

The gentlemen wear top hats and bowlers as was customary then, and to the right on the island, the young man with the light-coloured, strikingly striped trousers is right up-to-date. Cheerful and relaxed, chattering and flirting, the ladies and gentlemen squeezing on to the island and visiting the restaurant relish their leisure. In the foreground, weightless boats are bobbing as a child bends down towards them. A dog dozes comfortably in the sun. To the right on the wooden walkway, a boy with a swimming ring makes his way towards the bathers splashing in the Seine on the left. In the second half of the nineteenth century, water sports were no longer seen purely as therapeutic and had instead become a symbol of youthful abandon. In addition to rowing and bathing activities, the astute owner of La Grenouillère, Servin, also put on regattas and dances. So there was something for every taste: you could row, sail, swim, dance, have a picnic, or just do nothing.

In Renoir's paintings, the people seem to be at one with the world; they seem to throw themselves into the pleasure of the moment. And so *La Grenouillère* seems like an updated representation of a journey to the island of Cythera imagined by the French painter Antoine Watteau (page 20). Art historians discussing this work by Renoir have quite rightly pointed to Renoir's love of French Rococo painting and to Watteau's painting. But now ordinary citizens had access to pastimes that only the nobility had enjoyed in the eighteenth century. Mythically transfigured times had thus been transported through art into the present and kept alive in numerous illustrations. Now the young citizens were celebrating their own "fàtes galantes." In Renoir's own words: "In art, as in nature, what we are likely to think new is, at bottom, only a more or less modified continuation of what has gone before."[10] And yet, in Renoir's pictures – unlike those of Monet, Pissarro, and Sisley – human beings are always at the centre.

Short, broad, and separated brushstrokes, thickly applied, give the impression of the spontaneous immediacy of a painter working in situ. In this way, Renoir was able to capture the play of

La Grenouillère, 1869, detail

light on the leaves and on the moving surface of the water. At the same time, the visible motion of the brush and the avoidance of contours and conventional modelling created a new pictorial unity in which the different elements become part of one harmonious whole. A sense of space is no longer achieved through linear perspective, but through the layering of coloured planes which become smaller as they recede into depth. This technique was far removed from traditional practices where any traces of the process of painting, that is to say, individual brushstrokes and rough patches of dark and light, were to be smoothed out and rendered invisible. The Impressionists' style of painting was accordingly seen as provocative, in that the results looked like no more than sketches. But these separate brushstrokes did have a descriptive function determined by the material qualities of the object; thus,

Antoine Watteau
*Embarkation
for Cythera*, 1717

for example, horizontal brushstrokes would be used for water. The use of closely related tones and tonal values was also new and gave the works a coherence that prevails even under close scrutiny. Renoir's choice of colours was also influenced by the newest products in the range of portable tubes of paint that had been available since 1841, although, for example, the colour "viridian glow-

Lise, 1867

ing" had only been available since 1862.[11] Because of the unconventional technique Renoir had used for the Grenouillère pictures, he finally decided not to submit them to the Salon, which meant that, until the turn of the century, they were not known to the wider public. But these paintings – when all is said and done – may be cited as the beginnings of Impressionism, to which Renoir was to remain more or less faithful for the next decade.

Although Renoir had already experimented with new painting technique in the 1860's, it was now that he turned to everyday life for his subject matter. His new subjects in fact also corresponded to the aims of the realist movement led by Gustave Courbet, creating art that was truthful and accessible by virtue of being close to reality.

Claude Monet had enthusiastically told his fellow-students at Charles Gleyre's studio about this new way of looking at art which constituted a radical break with academic convention. Renoir's *Diana* (page 23) clearly shows the influence of Courbet's strict realism and his method of applying thick paint with a spatula.

Renoir's figures in the open air from before 1869 were by and large preparations for larger figure compositions, costume pieces or nudes. In the following years, which were to be the next most innovative of his œuvre after his work at La Grenouillère, Renoir took up themes from contemporary life in the modern city of Paris, where pleasure and entertainment were becoming ever more important.

Diana, 1867

Paris in the Belle Epoque

The Belle Epoque, as the decades preceeding World War I in France are evocatively called, represents more than any other period in French history the epitome of "savoir vivre," the art of enjoying life. On closer examination, and taking into account the fact that this period was, in reality, marked by workers' struggles, militant anarchist movements, ups and downs in the economy, crisis in the Church, and instable government, it may be that the glorious name given to this time is no more than a myth. Still, the general view of the Belle Epoque, and particularly of the decade from 1870 to 1880, is dominated by the notion of festivities and amusements. Just before the Third Republic (1870 – 1940), and during its early years, there were huge changes taking place on the cultural front, and countless new leisure pursuits were now open to Parisians of all classes.

Sound economic growth on the whole meant that by 1880 France was the first nation in Europe to have an established democracy, with the right to vote – albeit initially only for men – having been introduced in 1872. Liberal republicans not only demanded the right to work for all citizens, but also the right to education and to popular culture unhampered by hierarchical and religious ties. An ever broader and more varied middle class was now the backbone of society.

Against the background of a flourishing economy and the resulting increase in prosperity – industrial production trebled and the gross national income doubled – virtually rampant materialism set in and, along with it, a craving for mass-entertainment. The development of the railway network (with the Metro underground train system after 1900), proper roads linking the capital to the most important towns around the country, and the growing numbers of bicycles meant that individuals were now able to travel on a previously undreamt-of scale. An immense array of leisure activities, vigorously publicized by means of poster campaigns – another innovation – were now available to a much broader band of the population thanks to the advent of quick, cheap transport.

Les grands Boulevards,
1875, detail

25

Boulevard des
Capucines,
Photograph,
ca. 1890

The Third Republic brought with it new forms of mass-culture.
In Paris this meant the opening of large numbers of establish-
ments to entertain the public, some of which were very long-
lasting and – like the Folies-Bergère – still exist today. The most
popular places of entertainment were the Café-Concerts, also known
as "democratic theatres" or "poor folk's theatres." These were
generally simple cafés with a small stage and a few singers. Some
of these cafés were like English music halls with extremely varied
programmes and theatrical sets. The Folies-Bergère, with roughly
500,000 visitors a year, was one of those very popular establish-
ments, held up by supporters of the Republic as a sign of democratic progress, but decried by conservatives as vulgar and deca-
dent. Never before had so many country-folk, workers, and
members of the middle class been able to take part in social and
cultural events which had up until then been the exclusive pre-
serve of a small elite. Books, concerts, and the theatre were now
there for everyone. The education system, including free primary
schooling and public libraries, became an important forum for
the propagation of Republican values. And so when July 14 was
officially declared a public holiday in commemoration of the fall
of the Bastille, this act took on particular significance for all
French men and women – while street celebrations and proces-
sions inspired Edouard Manet, Claude Monet, and Camille Pissarro
to some unusual works.

26

Although it was still only the very few that were able to purchase a work of art or an automobile, and not everyone could afford to go public places of entertainment, prices were nevertheless kept so low that the majority of the population were able to take advantage of these. Even the luxury entertainments of the rich and the aristocracy, like the races at Longchamps and the bet-

Leopold Lelée
Folies-Bergère — Tous les Soirs Spectacle Varié,
Color lithograph

Pont-Neuf, Photograph,
ca. 1890, Archives Roger-Viollet

Right:
The Pont-Neuf, Paris, 1872

ting that went with them, were opened to the broad masses in the 1890s, as can be seen in many of Degas' works. On the other hand, a relatively expensive visit to the Paris Opera, the Opera Ball, or La Comédie Française could still only be contemplated by the elite, for a ticket to the opera cost about the same as an unskilled labourer would earn in a month. It was possible to see inside the opera house free of charge on one of its "open doors" days, but beyond this, the workers and the poor had their own, more afford-able Café-Concerts, dance halls, and places of entertainment.

Despite the government's efforts to establish liberal, repub-lican notions of culture, social barriers and privileges remained largely in place. Compared to the situation in Germany or Great Britain, and regardless of the fact that the socialist party had been founded in 1880, the proletariat's demands generally fell on deaf ears. Against a background of militant and anarchist movements which found little support among the broad masses, social re-forms on a national level were slow to take effect. The other side of this consumer- and pleasure-oriented time, which meant a higher standard of living above all for the middle classes, was a deep-seat-ed fear of national decline and the loss of cultural values. These fears were not only nourished by a background of social tension and political conflict, but also by the falling birth rate and the in-creasing independence of women. Concealed by the Third Repub-lic's cult of manhood, with its code of honour and duels, there was in fact a deep crisis between the sexes. Although women only gained the vote after the Second World War, they were already in-creasingly active in public life, despite the prevailing patriarchal view of woman's place as being strictly in the home.

But unlike Henri de Toulouse-Lautrec or Edgar Degas, Renoir ex-cluded the darker side of this glittering era from his works. His paintings depicting modern Parisian life, which he made until the early eighties, are witness to the "glittering" side of life. They con-sciously avoid any hint of toil or suffering. Speaking to the painter Jean-Franáois Raffaëlli, Renoir expressed his attitude to darker social issues with perfect clarity: "There are enough unpleasant things in the world. We don't have to paint them as well."[12]

But it would be simplistic to see the insatiable thirst for enter-tainment as no more than escapism, for it was the reflection of a

Pont des Arts, Paris, 1867

deep-seated sense of cultural unease at the time. Indeed Renoir's scenes of Parisian life, showing people seeking social contact, friendship, and love, are at the same time his vision of an organic society, of the harmonious union of humanity and nature. The "Golden Age" that this evokes is the antithesis of an epoch in which world-weary critics were preaching modesty and restraint. So it was the world of ordinary folk that fascinated Renoir – in contrast to Edouard Manet's scenes of fashionable Paris – and in his work he was always open to the fundamental changes in painting that matched the far-reaching social upheavals of the time.

Pierre-Auguste Renoir himself came from a petit-bourgeois background. His father was a tailor. The family was poor, so Auguste and the other children were obliged to go out to work from an early age. With a talent for drawing, he began an apprenticeship in porcelain painting and quickly became so good at it that he was soon painting figures – often nudes – and portraits onto the white porcelain. This kind of painting with soft, round brushes and clear,

31

transparent colours continued to interest Renoir throughout his life. But after a four-year apprenticeship, the invention of printed designs for porcelain meant that he had to look for other employment, and he found work painting fans. "So I began decorating fans with copies of Watteau, Lancret, and Boucher. I even used Watteau's *Embarkation for Cythera*! ... To be more precise, Boucher's *Diana at the Bath* was the first picture that took my fancy, and I have clung to it all my life as one does to one's first love."[13] Various commissions resulted from his skills as a decorator; they were profitable enough for him to save towards studying painting without initially giving up his work as a craftsman. "I had taken Venus rising from the waves for my subject. And I can assure you that I didn't spare either the Veronese green or the cobalt. ... I painted at least twenty cafés in Paris. ... How I would like to do decoration again, like Boucher, and transform entire walls into Olympuses. What a dream!"[14]

He copied the Old Masters in the Louvre – above all those of the seventeenth and eighteenth centuries – and enrolled in courses in l'Ecole des Beaux-Arts. From 1862 to 1864 he worked in Charles Gleyre's independent studio. Other young painters also preferred the independent studios because Salon art and thus, by implication, the relevant training in l'Ecole des Beaux-Arts, for them seemed false and somehow divorced from reality. Camille Pissarro, Paul Cézanne, and Armand Guillaumin had all attended the independent Académie Suisse, and now Renoir was studying alongside Claude Monet, Alfred Sisley, and Frédéric Bazille, with whom he became friends. Monet, first and foremost, won his friends over to the realism of Courbet. Although Gleyre himself subscribed to the prevalent ideals of beauty, he nevertheless viewed his students' realist theories with tolerance. He encouraged them to develop their own style and recommended working in the open air. So from 1862 onwards the four friends — Renoir, Bazille, Sisley, and Monet — painted outside in the Forest of Fontainebleau, in the very place where the Barbizon painters had previously founded their school of landscape painting.

Between 1830 and 1850, in the small village of Barbizon on the edge of the Forest of Fontainebleau, a group of painters had formed who rejected classical conventions in art. Their landscapes known as "paysages intimes" – drawing above all on seventeenth-

Parisienne, 1874

32

Narcisse Diaz de la Peña
The Forest near
Fontainebleau, 1874

century bourgeois Dutch landscape painting – set new standards of unpretentiousness and simplicity. In their desire to represent nature realistically and in a manner that anyone could understand, these painters – the precursors of Impressionism – found a way of working outside, although not all the time. This in itself owed much to the availability (since the 1840s) of oil paints in tubes. In the Barbizon school, nature itself was to stand answer, to be understood in its actual being, and to be depicted realistically. In fact, some of these landscape painters were later to become leading figures in the Impressionist movement, including Charles-François Daubigny (1817 – 1878), Narcisse Diaz de la Peña (1809 – 1876), Jules Dupré (1811 – 1899), Constant Troyon (1810 – 1865), and Camille Corot (1796 – 1875).

It was in 1862 in the Forest of Fontainebleau that Renoir first met Narcisse Diaz who advised him against using dark asphalt black. Diaz arranged credit terms for Renoir with his own paint-dealer and, in a friendly way, encouraged him to paint in the open air. And it was here in 1865 that Monet's *Le Déjeuner sur l'Herbe* (page 35) (Paris, Musée d'Orsay) came into being, a monumental figure composition painted from studies made in the open air. Unlike Monet, Sisley, and Pissarro, from the outset Renoir painted figures rather than landscapes. So, during his stay in the Forest of Fontainebleau, he set his sights on an equally ambitious undertaking in the form of the large figure composition, *The Cabaret of Mother Anthony* (page 37) (1866, Stockholm, Nationalmuseum), which also has echoes of Courbet, whose spatula technique Renoir had often adopted. Gustave Courbet led the movement of realist painters who were firmly opposed to any idealized, prettified representation of reality. Courbet's demands that a painting should be truthful, fitting for its own time, and socially meaningful was in keeping with Charles Baudelaire's concept of "new, modern painting" which also recognized simple, everyday themes as worthy of depiction. In the eyes of Baudelaire, critic and poet, this modern form of art, with its morals rooted in the present and freed from traditional archetypes, owed its central impulse to the new feeling in society, which he described as "l'héroisme de la vie moderne," and which he sensed above all in Paris.

Other thinkers were making similar demands for art, such as Duranty in the manifesto of 1876, "La Nouvelle Peinture": "So let us bid farewell to the stylized human form that is treated like a vase. What we need is characteristic, modern people in their own clothes, in the heart of their own social surroundings, at home or out in the street."[15]

Claude Monet
Le Déjeuner sur l'Herbe, 1865/66, central panel

35

The rejection of several major works by the Salon in 1855 spurred Courbet to put on a counter-exhibition during the World's Fair in the so-called "Pavillon du Réalisme." This move was enthusiastically supported by younger painters and was to prove seminal in its influence.

In 1863 the so-called "Salon des Réfusés" was of comparable importance. That year, the number of works rejected by the official Salon jury — including Renoir's *Nymphe* — had been unusually high. In response to the vociferous indignation which ensued, a separate exhibition was put on in the annexe to the Salon showing works by "les rejetés." And, as is well known, a scandal was created by Manet's *Le Déjeuner sur l'Herbe* which showed a nude young woman calmly regarding the viewer without embarrassment as she sits in the open air between two men dressed in fashions of the time. The rendering of the female nude here should have adhered to the ideals of academic tradition, as did Alexandre Cabanel's *Birth of Venus* which was exhibited in the Salon at the time and was bought by the emperor.

Familiarity with Manet's work reinforced not only Renoir's but all the Impressionists' own efforts to establish a modern form of painting: "Courbet was still in the tradition, whereas Manet belonged to a new era in painting."[16]

In view of the lack of opportunity to exhibit their works, in 1874 the Impressionists stepped into the public light with their first independent, privately organized exhibition, only to meet with scorn and opposition for their small-format, sketch-like, spontaneously-painted landscapes and simple scenes from everyday life. But only ten years later, their "revolutionary" style had won countless admirers and became the starting point for new directions in modern art. Despite certain reforms in its internal politics in the 1880s, the Salon gradually began to lose its importance, although it did retain its attraction for foreign artists.

Besides the special technique of visibly separate brushstrokes — which in academic terms marked a work out as a sketch — and the rejection of traditional light-dark contrasts to model forms in favour of a much more even range of tonal values, it was the new, unusual themes from contemporary everyday life that caused astonishment. The Impressionists did not only show landscapes,

The Cabaret of Mother Anthony, 1866

36

but also the pulsating city life of the boulevards and avenues, the restaurants, cafés, theatres, and dance halls. And yet, in spite of the similarity of their subject matter, individual painters very much pursued their own paths.

Renoir's *Les Grands Boulevards* of 1875, for example, is a typical picture of "modern life." It is not, however, the formless mass of the city (as in Monet's *Boulevard des Capucines*) that holds his interest, but rather an anecdotal view of individual scenes taken separately, as it were. In the left foreground, a man sits reading in front of a kiosk in the shade of the trees. On one side of the street, there are two men with top hats and an elegant lady accompanied by two children. An open carriage drives by on the right. Renoir shows the city in its "civilized garb."

Claude Monet
*Boulevard
des Capucines,*
1873/74

Les grands Boulevards, 1875

Paradise on Earth in Montmartre

The renewal of Paris that Napoleon III carried out with the Seine Prefect George Haussmann between 1853 and 1870 included, among other things, the construction of new representational buildings. One of the most imposing of these was the Paris Opera. And in addition, to this there were green areas like le Bois de Boulogne and le Bois de Vincennes[17] – inspired by English parks and generously laid out with all kinds of entertainments – oases of rest and recuperation for city-dwellers. Although areas of the city that would have been worth keeping were lost, the overall gains were unmistakable. Paris, which now took on the aspect of a modern city, with an image that radiated right across Europe, became the "capital city of the nineteenth century."

As far as Renoir was concerned, the main impetus behind "Haussmannization" was the general craving for profit, to which everything was sacrificed in order that land prices be pushed up. He hated the world of industrialists, bankers, and speculators, and often lamented the changes: "What have they done to my poor Paris! ... I love theatre settings, but in the theatre."[18] As part of the process of renewal, the surrounding parishes, some still very rural, were incorporated into the city. In 1860 this happened to the little village of Montmartre, set on a hill and making a living by its numerous mills, vineyards, and chalk quarries. The writer Gérard de Nerval described it as having been a real green oasis up until then: "There are mills, inns and summer houses, country areas and quiet lanes, lined with straw-sheds, barns and tree-filled gardens."[19] Those living there were predominantly peasants and workers because the rents were still cheap. In 1860 Montmartre only had 4,000 inhabitants but, after being incorporated into the city, it quickly became one of the most densely- populated parts of Paris. Attracted by its rural peace, numerous artists, poets, and musicians settled there in the eighties and the art business got under way.

With its outdoor pubs, taverns or "cabarets" (after 1878 "la Grande Pinte" was the best known), and dances, Montmartre be-

Le Moulin de la Galette, 1876, detail

41

came a favourite outing for city folk and created the reputation of "la butte" (the hillock) as a place of entertainment and pleasure. And the city scene was further enlivened by the many cafés and café-concerts on the great boulevards, (boulevard Rochechouart and boulevard de Clichy) and the squares, (place de Clichy, place Blanche, and place Pigalle).

Coffee houses had already been firmly established in Paris since the middle of the eighteenth century, and during the course of the nineteenth century the number of cafés selling other things besides coffee – such as alcohol and tobacco – increased by leaps and bounds. Cafés became centres for communication and discussion, important meeting places for Parisian society. The Impressionists met in le Café Guerbois and later in le Café de la Nouvelle-Athènes to discuss their theories. Thus public spaces became private. The scene in the painting, *Studio in rue Saint-Georges* (page 116), showing Renoir with his friends Rivière, Pissarro, Lestringuez, and Cabanel could just as easily have been set in a café. Sitting in a window seat, the customer in a café could play the observer and take part in the "drama of life" just as though he or she were visiting the theatre with a blurring of the boundaries between a person's private inner space and the public, outside world.

A particular curiosity was the Circus Fernando: Renoir captured the artistry of its performers in his picture of the same name (page 43) and it was here in Montmartre that Renoir found the source of his inspiration for his city paintings.

In around 1870, the number of public dances in Paris was so great that guides to the city would set aside several pages to list them all. There were so many opportunities that it seemed that in Paris dancing was a necessity of life. Balls were held not only in dance halls but also in the open air in squares, courtyards, parks, and streets. The masked ball at the Opera became an important social event. Although after 1850 these entertainments were commercialized to a large extent – such as the "le Bal Mabille" – the dances in the suburbs and outlying districts retained much of their popular character and were mainly for the working classes (and soldiers). So the rag-and-bone merchants had their "Bal du Vieux-Chène," the washerwomen and women from the market stalls had

Jugglers at the Cirque Fernando, 1879

PARIS (Vieux-Montmartre). — Impasse Girardon

Facing Page: View of the slums behind the mills operated by the Debray family; Postcard, ca. 1870

The old quarter around the Montmartre, Moulin de la Galette; Postcard, ca. 1870

Right:
Moulin de la Galette; Postcard, ca. 1870

192 — PARIS - Moulin de la Galette

B. F., PARIS

Dancing at the Moulin
de la Galette, ca. 1900;
Photograph, Archives
Roger–Viollet

"le Grand Salon Ragache," and the artists in Montmartre had the
"Casino" in rue Cadet.

One of the most typical dance-bars in Montmartre was le
Moulin de la Galette, also known as "le Radet." Originally it had
been one of fourteen mills on Montmartre which had been in operation since the sixteenth century.[20] The building and the nearby
"scenic-view mill," (pages 44 / 45) with a telescope that afforded a
wonderful view of Paris for 10 centimes, belonged to the Debray
family. In 1838, the mill – at that time milling iris roots for the
Paris perfume industry instead of flour – was transformed by Père
Debray into an almost instantly successful dance-bar.[21] An outdoor dance-floor, seen in the background of Renoir's painting
(page 53), was added to the simple inn, named after the "galettes"
(round waffles) it was now selling along with cheap red wine, instead of the bread and milk from before. Here on sunny Sunday
afternoons people danced under the acacias – as described by
Georges Rivière.[22]

Renoir and his artist friends were regularly to be found there.
Music was provided by an orchestra of "ten poor devils" playing on
a raised podium. In the evenings the garden was atmospherically
lit by round gas-lamps, those "artificial suns" of the industrial
age. [23] Encouraged by his friend Franc-Lamy, who had discovered
a study of *Le Moulin de la Galette* in Renoir's studio (perhaps the

sketch now in the Museum in Copenhagen), Renoir painted a large canvas full of figures on this subject in 1875.

In 1875, a commission for a "princely sum," the *Portrait of Madame Charpentier and her Children*, enabled him to rent two rooms (without giving up his flat in rue Saint-Georges) in the second storey of an old building in rue Cortot on the idyllic north side of the hill of Montmartre, near to le Moulin de la Galette, so he would be able to paint on site in the afternoons. This decrepit building, which now houses the Montmartre Museum, had already long been in use as artists' studios. Behind it there was an overgrown garden with a magnificent view out over the plain

Portrait of Madame Charpentier and her Children, 1878

of Saint-Denis. Renoir called it the "mysterious garden" and compared it to Zola's Paradou, itself the remains of a previously grand home. In this oasis he produced not only the first studies for *Le Moulin de la Galette* but also *The Swing* (page 55), pictures of the actress Jeanne Samary (page 65), *Nude in the Sunlight* (page 58), and *La Première Sortie* (page 77).

The dense, layered composition of *Le Moulin de la Galette* along with the later *Luncheon of the Boating Party* was to become one of Renoir's most significant works. Renoir found the models for the earlier painting at le Moulin de la Galette itself. The two young women in the foreground of the work, Jeanne and Estelle – seamstresses without fixed employment, known as "grisettes" – are dressed in the latest fashions. They wear their light brown hair up in chignons with fringes or bangs (favoured above all by young girls) and decorated with Parma violets and a hair-net à la napolitaine finished with pearls, fringes, and tassels. None of the girls or women are dressed in the typical wide, tucked-up dresses and short-sleeved blouses that working women used to wear. While contemporary authors and painters like Degas depicted the poverty of these girls, who frequently possessed neither corsets nor underclothes, Renoir glossed over their threadbare aspect and gave them a dignified appearance.

After about 1860, Parisians in every walk of life made an effort to dress particularly smartly on Sundays. Workers would slip into the role of the bourgeoisie and fashion trends followed one another with ever increasing rapidity. But this meant that fine society ladies were quickly overtaken in their dress by women from the "twilight regions" with the result that modest restraint now became the true sign of elegance.

Sitting with his back to the viewer at the table in the right foreground, the painter Désiré Eugène Franc-Lamy (1855 – 1919) has been identified, along with Norbert Goeneutte smoking a pipe (1854 – 1894), Georges Rivière with writing materials, and, dancing in the centre, Marguerite ("Margot") Legrand, a girl from the quarter (page 57) with the Spanish painter Pedro Vidal de Solarès (with his Calabrian felt hat). The dancers also include the painters Henri Gervex (1852 – 1929), Frédéric Cordey (1854 – 1911), and the art-

Le Moulin de la Galette, 1876 (Preliminary sketch)

lovers Pierre-Eugène Lestringuez (a journalist), and Paul Lhote. Contented children (in the lower left-hand corner of the painting) – as in *The Swing* – embody the paradisaical innocence of the scene for, according to Renoir, a child's view of the world is the happiest.

The people in Renoir's *Le Moulin de la Galette* are clearly enjoying the pleasures of being young, in good health, and, as yet, unworn by life's cares. And at the same time, the dance itself is a quite particular expression of individuals that are at ease with themselves and enjoying a growing sense of physical freedom.[24] In le Moulin de la Galette they danced Viennese waltzes which allowed the dizzying sensation of body contact, while in the quadrilles and contradances in the other dance halls, only the hands or the fingertips were permitted to touch.

The structure of this work displays the typical characteristics of Impressionist composition: the figures to the left and the right in the foreground are cut abruptly off by the edge of the picture, so that viewers have the feeling that they have an actual slice of reality in front of them which continues beyond the picture frame. Renoir may have subconsciously absorbed ideas from contemporary photography and from Japanese woodcuts, so often referred to in connection with Impressionism, but he emphatically denied any direct influence: "Photography is going to kill the amateur painter and, indirectly, the art-lover; and it may even kill the painter since the art-lover is his source of livelihood."[25] And elsewhere: "Japanese prints are certainly most interesting, as Japanese prints ... that is to say, on condition they stay in Japan."[26]

The rapid decrease in the size of the brushstrokes draws the viewer's gaze from the figures in close-up in the foreground to the individual dancing couples in the centre of the picture and yet further into the background, where single dabs of colour merely sketch in more figures. Coloured light and shade seem to be dispersed across the picture purely for their own sake. Thus the round patches of light on the jacket of the figure in the foreground sitting with his back to the viewer have a strange life all of their own. Indistinct brushstrokes and violet shadows are superimposed on each other and there is a blue tone uniting the different parts of the picture. If one is to accept a contemporary review of this work, it is as though the solidly physical figures have been showered with "Impressionist confetti." But to speak of this painting as a spontaneous and immediate response to the motif would be incorrect since many studies for this work exist, including detailed studies for the different poses of the dancing couples which were then worked into the final composition in the studio. In his not always entirely accurate memoirs, Georges Rivière writes of a large-format study which was apparently executed entirely outside and was carried by Renoir with the help of his friends backwards and forwards between the Moulin de la Galette and the studio in rue Cortot.[27] The other known version of the motif, which once belonged to the New York art collector Whitney (and is now in a private collection in Japan), is surely a replica Renoir made for the collector Victor Chocquet from the final version of

Le Moulin de la Galette, 1876, detail

50

the painting, which now hangs in the Musée d'Orsay in Paris. The whereabouts of the study described by Rivière and therefore the proof for the existence, are therefore open to speculation.

A comparison with Jules Pelocq's illustration from a news journal [28] shows that Renoir's record of the scene is much more dynamic and complex. Unlike other contemporary depictions of fashionable balls, such as Manet's *Opera Ball* or *Concert in the Tuileries*, Renoir's *Le Moulin de la Galette* conveys the pleasurable side of bourgeois aspirations without making a detailed examination of the underlying psychology.

As a painter, Renoir was not interested in rigidly applying Impressionist techniques which, in their rejection of the conventions of figure painting, constituted a radical break with traditions handed

Le Moulin de la Galette,
1876 (New York version)

Le Moulin de la Galette,
1876 (Paris version)

down since the days of the Renaissance. Only a few of his pictures from the seventies are in line with Impressionist techniques in the strict sense. Renoir made it clear from the outset that, for him, a modern, innovative work did not by definition have to go against what had been inherited from the Renaissance. Thus, while he portrayed themes from modern life, he drew from time-honoured principles for his understanding of aesthetics. Renoir was most definitely not among the revolutionary pioneers of modernism, instead seeming much more like a mediator between change and tradition.

These apparent contradictions also characterize the picture of the artist himself that various sources – in particular Renoir's son Jean – have passed on to us. His unease regarding his own social status, his anxiety about his position as an artist, and his clearly ambivalent attitude towards women might well have counted among "those strange contradictions which made his reasoning

53

difficult to understand."[29] Upholding traditions meant a lot to Renoir – in his personal life too – and doing so became increasingly important to him as he grew older.

Simply dressed and of necessity making a principle of a modest life-style, Renoir quickly became an established figure in Montmartre and felt an affinity with its inhabitants through his own petit-bourgeois background. He regarded himself as a painter from the working lower-middle class and was only too well aware that his pictures bored some patrons and art-lovers from the upper class. In these circles[30] his careless dress, his inadequate table manners and social graces, and his nervousness were all criticized, and he felt correspondingly ill at ease in such society and in the affected, ethereal atmosphere of the city's salons. In strong contrast, however, to his nervous inner tension[31] are his harmonious, calm, almost timeless works such as *Le Moulin de la Galette* or *The Swing*. In these paintings, Renoir offers the viewer his vision of unrestrained social interaction in a relaxed, sensual atmosphere — of a togetherness unbound by social convention and norms. But at the same time, these pictures reflect Renoir's own attitude to life. His advice to behave "badly" before marriage (!) and to try out new kinds of relationships was directed to men and women alike.[32] In the 1870s Renoir himself had several affairs with different women from the working class who, like Lise Tréhot (1848 – 1922) and Margot Legrand (d. 1879) also sat as models for him.

The young girls of Montmartre who posed as models for him were by no means entirely virtuous. The morals in that quarter of the city were not particularly strict and the area was swarming with children who did not know their fathers. The high number of unmarried men and women in Paris in the nineteenth century meant that many were seeking relationships before marriage,[33] and in the poorer quarters of the towns, these arrangements would seem to have been commonplace. There was widespread prostitution – described by Emile Zola in his novel *Nana* as a new form of darkly enticing temptation – and coquettish women were much in demand. Following the noticeable liberalization of love in France since the 1860s, seduction became an everyday matter with romantic love only to be found in novels and stage-plays.

The Swing, 1876

54

The Arbour, 1875

Like his male contemporaries, Renoir only saw women as fit for particular traditional roles and spheres of operation; as the "ideal" woman – the Madonna – she fitted easily into the male world-view, while as the "new Eve," as a shameless, ravening beast – and temptress – she was supposedly instrumental in the downfall of men (and of society). Unlike many other artists and writers of the day, Renoir did not take up this image of the "all-devouring female" in any of his paintings. On the contrary, in the few nudes that he painted in the seventies, he portrayed the lighter side of womanhood. Renoir's *Nude in the Sunlight*, also known as *Torso d'Anna* (page 58) conveys something of this response to the nude form that is both pleasurable and natural without being provocative. This nude, which was compared to Fragonard's *Bather*, shows woman as both alluring and unattainable, and demonstrates a degree of typical modesty and reticence on the part of the artist, who saw himself as extremely shy. It would probably never have occurred to him to expose the female form as Degas had done in his *Bathers*. For Renoir the nude female figure – above all in his late

Margot, 1876/77

works – is a metaphor for beauty, truth, and purity. Talking to Julie Manet in 1898[34], he recalled his frequent visits to le Moulin de la Galette where all the Montmartre families would meet each other, and described how he was struck by "the degree of sensitivity amongst people from such simple backgrounds, whom Zola spoke of as awful people." He was much taken by their sense of freedom: "It was 'never a gross kind of liberty' they indulged in, or any licence".[35] It goes almost without saying that Renoir's carefree picture of city dwellers in his *Le Moulin de la Galette* did not reflect the reality of everyday life. Poverty and misery were to be found in their true colours just a few metres behind the mill in the worst of makeshift dwellings and other scandalous living quarters. In his memories of the life of Toulouse-Lautrec, François Gauzi describes the mill on Sunday afternoons as always being "a worthy place," but goes on to say that in the evening it was so dangerous that he would avoid going there with Toulouse-Lautrec.[36] Renoir was simply transposing his persistent notion of an "earthly paradise," of a sociable, harmonious society in which class differences were of no significance, onto the hill of Montmartre in the Paris of the 1870s.

Paul Lhote, a close friend of Renoir's, creates a poetic image of this paradise on Montmartre in his short story of 1883, "Mademoiselle Zélia."[37] The protagonist is the painter Resmeer, easily identifiable as Renoir. Resmeer rents – like Renoir – a studio in rue Cortot in Montmartre where he paints "nymph-like beings" under trees, beings that he finds personified in some of the young girls of that quarter. Resmeer wanted to portray the carefree time of life and therefore preferred to surround himself with young people. The painter's garden quickly became a favourite meeting place, a "hortus conclusus" where pretty young girls would wander like nymphs and it seemed possible that the sexes could be as one. And in fact this all seems to have distinct similarities with Renoir's own garden in rue Cortot.

Behind this vision of Renoir's lay his desire for a world without regulation, urbanization, industrialization and depersonalization. He saw his ideal of an organic, Arcadian society realized in the paintings of Antoine Watteau, François Boucher, and Honoré Fragonard. "Presumably the taste that comes to us from the pictures of the eighteenth century is rooted in our subconscious: we are

Nude in the Sunlight
(Torso d'Anna), 1875/76

never consciously aware of human achievements!"[38] This enthusiasm for the eighteenth century was also reflected in the court of the Empress Eugénie and in the preference for rococo costumes at the famous masked balls.

Renoir was convinced that there was no stopping the destruction of values handed down from the eighteenth century which he held so dear, and so in his *Le Moulin de la Galette*, as before in *La Grenouillère* – both timelessly modern yet with echoes of Watteau – he created his own personal version of the immortal isle of Cythera. Renoir, who himself came from modest circumstances, knew the hard daily grind of simple, working people, and in showing them on celebration days and holidays, he transfigured their lives and lent them "nobility" through their grace and beauty. In comparison to the tense images of Paris by Manet and Degas, which dealt with the bitter, unattractive side of life – in a distanced, reserved, sometimes even cynical manner – Renoir's works may seem less compelling to the modern-day viewer, and yet they do bear witness to their creator's true human feeling and warmth.

Garden in rue Cortot,
1876

"He has painted the woman of Paris"

Paul Cézanne

Paris offered Renoir a rich setting for his paintings: with the brightly-lit shop-windows as the backdrop, the streets as the stalls, and the passers-by as the audience. In journals of the day, the metropolis is described as a theatre, "richly decorated and fantastically illuminated at night. ... Everywhere there were glittering shops, sumptuous displays, gold encrusted cafés and permanent lighting. ... As you stroll along you can read a newspaper by the light streaming from the shop windows."[39]

"The gas chandeliers sparkle and the floating lamps glow and ... the transparent illuminated advertising tells in huge fiery letters of the wonders of the Parisian night and the crowds of people flow to and fro."[40] Behind the scenes, it was the women of Paris who ruled over this glamorous world.

Fashion, changing season by season, defined a new form of femininity – making a statement not only about a woman's social standing, but also about her personality and character. With the development of ready-made clothing and the invention of fashion shows and mannequins, fashion also became an important sector of the economy in its own right. The newly-established department stores, where affordable clothes could be bought off the rack,[41] became nothing less than shopping paradises, as Zola described them in his novel *Au Bonheur des Dames*,[42] which Renoir illustrated (page 64). And women from the middle and the working classes also had access to this commercialized world of fashion in a development which Renoir viewed with open criticism: "You see, the trouble with ready-made clothing is that everybody can afford to look well-dressed – as well-dressed as a commercial traveller. You have the workman disguised as a gentleman, for the modest price of twenty-five francs fifty. When I was a youngster, workmen were proud of their profession. ... Now they've replaced pride in their profession by this idiotic vanity of trying to look like the bourgeoisie. In consequence, the streets of Paris seem to be filled with supers out of a play by the younger Dumas."[43]

La Loge, 1874

Illustration for Zola's
Au bonheur des Dames,
1883, engraving

Renoir's *Parisienne* of 1874 (page 33), with her high neckline, her
capote hat and her gloves, seems shy and reserved. Although her
delicately painted, intense blue, mauve-tinged dress and S-shaped
silhouette as well as her overall doll-like appearance are all the
latest fashion,[44] she does not have that final touch of chic, modish-
ness, and elegance that marks comparable paintings like perhaps
Edouard Manet's self-assured *Parisienne* (Ellen Andrée), of 1875.

The model for Renoir's *Parisienne* was most probably the young
actress Henriette Henriot, who had been one of his favourite
models since 1874. In *Studying a Role* (page 66), Renoir does
not show her in one of her stage roles, but instead in the company
of Georges Rivière (in the foreground) and Renoir's brother
Edmond. Similarly in the portraits of the actress *Jeanne Samary*
(page 67) who appeared at le Théâtre Français, the subject's
professional activities would seem to be without any significance.
In Jeanne Samary's case, Renoir was captivated by her pale skin,
her aura of sensuality, and her femininity, for along with generous
curves and a warmly gleaming profusion of hair, white skin was
taken as the hallmark of female beauty. According to Renoir himself, he wanted to "paint human beings like fruits."

Edouard Manet
*Parisienne: Dress with a
Train*, 1875

Facing Page:
*Portrait of the Artist
Jeanne Samary,* 1878

64

Studying a Role, 1874

Jeanne Samary, 1877

Top:
Madame Charpentier,
1876/77

*Berthe Morisot and her
Daughter,* 1894

68

Young Woman Braiding her Hair, 1876

With a few exceptions such as Degas' *Women Ironing*, the depiction of women hard at work was not a motif favoured by the Impressionists. The working women they portrayed came mainly from the world of cabaret and the theatre. The viewing public – men and women alike – were fascinated by singers, actresses, and dancers, who were a rich source of artistic inspiration not only for painters.

In keeping with male-dominated attitudes of this sort, Renoir painted his friend, the Impressionist painter *Berthe Morisot* and the open-minded *Madame Charpentier* (page 68) – with her republican leanings, and whose salon was frequented by artists, poets, intellectuals, and feminists – both in their roles as mothers, although this did not signify any less respect for them on his part. Morisot's tender images of girls, young women, and children fitted exactly his ideal of femininity. "My friendship with her [Madame Morisot] has been one of the finest I have ever had. ... a painter so impregnated with the grace and delicacy of the eighteenth century; she was the last elegant and 'feminine' artist that we have had since Fragonard ..."[45]

The Young Woman Reading an Illustrated Journal (page 73) is apparently completely absorbed by a fashion journal. At the time of the Third Republic, public lending libraries sprang up specializing in light, trivial reading matter. While they did offer easier, less restricted access to books, at the same time they discouraged the practice of reading aloud. Within the boundaries of the home, reading opened up a "window on the world" as for the *Woman Reading* (page 70). Later on, Renoir even said to his son Jean that he much preferred women who could not read at all: "Why teach women such boring occupations as law, medicine, science and journalism, which men excel in, when women are so fitted for a task which men can never dream of attempting, and that is to make life bearable."[46]

Women's sphere of operation was the home, the children and the emotions, for according to contemporary patriarchal attitudes a woman did not think; on the contrary, she felt and – like children and wild creatures – her knowledge was instinctive. Playing the piano, for example, was an acceptable way for women to express their feelings. They were excluded from the abstract world of the

Woman Reading,
ca. 1876

71

Lady at the Piano, ca. 1875

intellect. Yet it would be wrong to accuse Renoir of misogyny. Like many men, he was convinced that he was doing women a favour by keeping them from the harsh realities of everyday life, and his statements on this count became increasingly rigid as he grew older.

Renoir's young women in *At the Café* (page 75), in *La Première Sortie* (page 77), or in *La Loge* (page 62) are never exposed to tricky, awkward situations as, for example, in Manet's *Chez le Père Lathuille* (page 74) where the restaurant owner's son is openly flirting with a female customer. The man seems to be taking total possession of the space occupied by the girl until she succumbs to his advances.

The Young Woman Reading an Illustrated Journal, 1880/81

*After the
Luncheon,*
1879

Above:
Edgar Degas, *Absinthe,* 1876

Left:
Edouard Manet, *Chez le Père Lathuille,*1879

At the Café, ca. 1877/78

Nini Lopez was probably Renoir's model for the scene *At the Café*. Although a male customer has already set his sights on her (with Georges Rivière, apparently, in the background), the outcome of the situation is completely open. And in the harmonious togetherness of the people in *After the Luncheon* (page 74), there are no hints of dissonance or of the doubts about the new urban reality that Manet or Degas clearly express in similar coffee-house scenes.

La Première Sortie of 1876 (page 77), like a snap-shot with the focus in the foreground, leads the viewer's gaze out into the auditorium. Since theatre boxes had movable chairs and their own entrance from the passage behind, one could either remain unrecognized in the shadows or, leaning over the balustrade, attract attention to oneself. Renoir shows a young girl, modestly and decently dressed, enjoying a visit to the theatre in the company of an older woman. The girl avoids the viewer's direct gaze by show-

La Loge,
ca. 1874

La Première Sortie, 1876

ing only her pretty profile. The public in the boxes opposite is only sketchily indicated. Here is the same carefully cherished innocence as in Renoir's youthful *Dancer* (page 79).

In contrast *La Loge* (page 62), from two years earlier, creates a very different effect, for here the protagonist self-confidently puts her femininity on display. This painting was shown at the first Impressionist exhibition in 1874 and is one of the most important works in this series. The theatre box itself becomes the scene of the drama. The woman's male companion, probably Renoir's brother Edmond, has gallantly left his lady the seat at the front and, from the depths of the box, is now observing those present through his opera glasses.

The depiction here of the latest fashions is of some significance, because men liked to demonstrate their own success by means of the jewellery and clothes worn by their women. Nini, known by the nickname "Gueule-de-Raie" (fish-mouth), wears a silk dress with broad stripes and trimmed in fur, with a swathe of pearls decorating the deeply-cut, lace-edged neckline. In her pinned-up hair the "Maiden of Montmartre" wears a simple white flower instead of a diadem. From the colour of her lips it seems that she is wearing lipstick, although in those days it was only "twilight" women that used lipstick, rouge, and eyebrow pencils.

The painterly treatment of the materials is striking here, with the contrast between silkily shimmering white and velvety black – for Renoir the "queen" of colours – taking up the play between light and dark. The viewer's gaze travels across the diagonal lines of the balustrade, the woman's arms slightly bent at the elbows, and the male companion, always coming back to Nini's charming face, whose "profile of antique purity" makes the painting a hymn of praise to natural feminine beauty.

Dancer, 1874

"A perpetual holiday and a mix of all classes"

Auguste Renoir

Luncheon of the Boating Party (1880/82) shows Renoir returning to idea of a large scale, busy figure composition, and is of comparable importance to the similarly sized *Le Moulin de la Galette*. Both paintings were started in the open air and completed in the studio. *After the Luncheon* (page 74) and *On the Terrace* (page 83) can be seen as their counterparts in terms of subject matter.

Between *Le Moulin de la Galette* (1876) and *Luncheon of the Boating Party* (1881) lie five years during which Renoir was working intensively on new themes that fitted the times, as well as further developing his technique as a painter. It was at this time that Renoir took up contact with the circle of Impressionists, although he did not adopt all of their views. Until 1878 he took part in their exhibitions with modest success while at the same time continuing to try (until 1890) to have his work accepted by the Paris Salon. Towards the end of the seventies, he became increasingly doubtful about the Impressionists' way of painting. This not only coincided with a period of change in his own personal life, but also with a time of general crisis in the Impressionist movement as a whole: "I had wrung Impressionism dry, and I finally came to the conclusion that I neither knew how to paint nor draw. In a word, Impressionism was a blind alley, as far as I was concerned."[47]

In 1880, Impressionism reached a turning point. After that, some painters not only declined to participate in the group exhibitions, but also openly turned to other movements, such as Symbolism. In order to find his way back to a stronger pictorial structure, Renoir took stock again of the Old Masters, and this meant that his work in the studio – which had always better suited Renoir the figure-painter – regained its former importance: "Light plays too great a part outdoors; you have no time to work out the composition; you can't see what you are doing."[48] In 1881, the search for new motifs that this change in orientation brought with it took him to Algeria for the first time. There he met up with Lhote, Lestringuez, and Cordey. Following this, he then went on to Italy, accompanied for some weeks by Aline Charigot, and then to the French

Luncheon of the Boating Party, 1880/81, detail

81

Mediterranean coast in 1882. Since 1880, regular purchases of his work by the Parisian gallerist Paul Durand-Ruel had eased his financial worries.

Although the southern light and luscious colours of the land-scapes he painted after this show his enthusiasm for Algeria, it was Italy that he loved. He was impressed above all by Raphael's frescoes in the Vatican and the wall-paintings of Pompeii, in par-ticular for their balanced composition, their clear lines, and the simplicity of their subject matter. Before he set off for Italy, he had already made an intensive study of oil-painting techniques in the manner of Jean-Auguste-Dominique Ingres, showing his newly awakened interest in drawing and pictorial line. It is possible that even before his departure he knew Cennino Cennini's handbook on Florentine painting in the fifteenth century which, among other things, describes fresco techniques, and which gave him the idea of writing a handbook of his own, although he never carried this out. In a later conversation, he was to say at one point that his jour-ney to Italy had made him recognize how a simpler palette could produce a richer effect. At the same time, it was in the south that he discovered his love of mythological themes.

Although his final break with the Impressionists did not take place until after he had been to Algeria and Italy — that is to say after 1883 — there had already been signs earlier on of his break with Impressionism. The comparison between *Le Moulin de la Galette* and *Luncheon of the Boating Party* is of considerable significance on this count.

The *Luncheon* shows a finite number of figures, each portrayed with his or her own individuality, with a sudden diminution in the size of the figures from foreground to background. While the different parts of *Le Moulin de la Galette* are held together by the same blue colour with the individuality of the figures subordin-ated to the collective identity of the group as a whole, in the *Lun-cheon* it is striking how very many different colours there are. And this lively spread of colour is matched by the juxtaposition of small, fine brushstrokes and broader, flatter ones. Even more than the complementary colours used (violet-blue and yellow, orange and blue), white plays a central role as a unifying agent. Thus the

On the Terrace, 1881

Eugène Le Poutevin
Near Etretat, 1865

various figures are distinct from each other, with Renoir bringing out their individuality. In the *Luncheon*, the line and solid forms created by traditional light-dark contrasts regain their former importance. Renoir had already begun to develop in this direction in the late seventies in his work on numerous portraits which required precise detail in order to achieve the required level of accuracy in the sitter's features.

Restaurant
Fournaise
on the Island
of Chatou,
Collection Sirou,
Paris

On the occasion of the Salon of 1880, Emile Zola urged Impressionist painters to progress, at long last, beyond what looked like sketches and to direct their efforts into more ambitious, more meaningful works from modern life. And his comments sound as though they might have been just the encouragement needed for the Luncheon, which was started shortly afterwards: "The style is there, infinitely fragmented. … [I]f one is easily satisfied, if one delivers work that is neither finished nor dry, then one loses interest in lengthy, carefully worked out pieces …" Therefore in future the Impressionists should "devote themselves to significant works that take years to work out."[49]

Restaurant Fournaise;
Photograph,
Archiv Chaumet, Paris

The setting for the boating party's relaxed enjoyment of each other's company is the Restaurant Fournaise on the Ile de Chatou, a neighbouring island to l'Ile de Croissy where the Grenouillère paintings had come into being in 1868. Monsieur Alphonse Fournaise ("le grand amiral"), a former boat-builder from Bougival, had started to serve refreshments for Sunday visitors and had constructed his own landing stage for the many Parisian water-sports enthusiasts where he – himself a keen water-sportsman – hired out boats and organised regattas. Having become comfort-

*Luncheon
of the Boating Party,*
1880/81

ably well off, he then had a three-storey stone house built which not only provided a home for his family, but also contained the Restaurant Fournaise. This quickly became a kind of club, with a relaxed atmosphere that Renoir greatly appreciated. "I remember an amusing restaurant there called Fournaise's, where life was a perpetual holiday. The world knew how to laugh in those days."[50] This was also where Renoir and Aline Charigot used to meet. Renoir had met the young seamstress from Montmartre in autumn 1880. The Restaurant Fournaise was easily reached from Renoir's studio in rue Saint-Georges, with a train leaving Saint-Lazare station every half hour for Saint-Germain and stopping at the station in Chatou.

The members of the boating party sit on the restaurant's terrace. Since the different figures are for the most part friends and acquaintances of Renoir's and could not always sit for him at the same time, the "cursed" picture took a long time to complete, and Renoir used individual studies to finish it off in the studio.

The viewer's attention is drawn first to the opulently laden table. A bowl with exotic fruits, half-full bottles, emptied glasses, and the remains of food all point to the end of a generous, shared meal. Sitting to the left of the table, Aline plays tenderly with her little dog. Behind her stands Alphonse Fournaise (it is not clear whether junior or senior) looking at a young woman (perhaps Alphonsine Fournaise) who leans on the railing of the terrace and listens to Baron Raoul Barbier sitting opposite her. The young man behind her (perhaps Alphonse Fournaise junior) is deep in conversation with the banker and art patron Charles Ephrussi (in the top hat). In the foreground, to the right of the table – opposite Aline – is the painter Gustave Caillebotte (astride his chair) and the actress Ellen Andrée with the Italian journalist Maggiolo bending down towards her.

In the background Paul Lhote (with the pince-nez) and Eugène Pierre Lestringuez (with the bowler hat) are turning playfully to the actress Jeanne Samary. She is either coquettishly covering her ears because the two gallants are making advances to her (Lhote already has a possessive hold on her waist) or she is adjusting her hat. At a second table in the middle ground of the picture the beautiful Angèle, a flower girl from Montmartre, enjoys her wine; the man in profile next to her could be Renoir's brother Edmond.[51]

Luncheon of the Boating Party, 1880/81, detail

88

As in *Le Moulin de la Galette*, members of different classes come together here in complete harmony: painters, actresses, journalists, civil servants, girls from Montmartre, ordinary citizens. They are united by shared pleasure and the happiness of the moment. The luscious green of nature around them, which only affords a small glimpse of other rowing boats and the banks of the Seine, thus cutting the scene off from the outside world, underlines the Arcadian quality of the scenery, and there is much greater eroticism here than in the comparatively harmless atmosphere at *Le Moulin de la Galette*. The couples seem to know each other; meaningful looks and signs of affection pass from one to the other.

Because of its celebratory character and the sense of unity between the figures, this work had been compared to Veronese's *Wedding at Canaa*.

The Boaters, 1880/81

Days under the Trees at the River

Argenteuil, Asnières, Bougival, Chatou and Croissy – all on the banks of the Seine – became a kind of Eldorado for Parisians in their leisure time. Excursions into the country were among their favourite pursuits. They transferred their "festivities" to the country with the result that the invasion of pleasure-seeking city-dwellers quickly made considerable inroads into what had once been an idyllic setting. Asnières, for instance, was only fifteen minutes away from Saint-Lazare by train and in the mid-nineteenth century was one of the most popular destinations for a day out, but tourism and the industry in the nearby city soon made it a less attractive place.

Although Renoir's *Boats on the Seine* (pages 96 / 97) of 1879 is also known by the name *The Seine at Asnières*, it was presumably not painted in situ. Even if there is controversy about the exact location, there still is a clear link with the scenes of boats that Renoir made in the Chatou area in the late 1870s.

Boating parties on the Seine were particularly favoured by pleasure-hungry Parisians as a weekend pastime, and by Impressionist artists as subject matter. Together with Monet in Argenteuil in 1874, Renoir painted several scenes of sailboats.

While Gustave Caillebotte, for example – himself an enthusiastic rower and yachtsman – represents rowing as a powerful, manly sport (page 98), Renoir's elegant amateur female rowers, without any visible signs of exertion, allow their boat to drift close to the bank in the warm light of a summer's day. In the centre of the composition there is the longed-for coming-together of nature and human beings, the unity of woman and water "as the origin of undivided being."[52] This "dissolving in water" is reflected in the small brushstrokes that link all the parts of the picture equally together. There are no linear divisions. Simultaneous colour contrasts like the orange of the boat as opposed to the orange and green of the vegetation increase the intensity of the colour and the light. In *Boats on the Seine*, Renoir comes close to Impressionism in an unusually uncompromising manner. He uses opaque, almost

Oarsmen in Chatou,
1879, detail

Oarsmen in Chatou, 1879

The Rowing-Boat, 1878 – 80

Overleaf: *Boats on the Seine (Seine at Asnières)*, 1879

unmixed colours without earth pigments or black, that is to say, a palette reduced to no more than six or seven colours (cinnabar, madder lake, viridian green, cobalt blue, chrome yellow or orange, lemon or Naples yellow).

Oarsmen in Chatou (page 94) comes from the same year. On the shores of the Ile de Chatou with a view towards Reuil, an unknown young woman stands between Caillebotte and a boy in a sailor costume. It has often been supposed that she is Aline Charigot, but Renoir only met his future wife a year later. In front of them, an oarsman has manoeuvred his two-man canoe to the shore, perhaps to take one of them with him as a passenger. On the Seine,

Top:
Frédéric Bazille, *Summer Scene, Bathers*, 1869

Right:
Gustave Caillebotte, *Périssoires (Rowers)*, 1878

Return of a Boating Party,
1862

two sporty one-man canoes pass by; a sailboat and a barge are headed up-stream. And here too the figures seem to merge with the surrounding vegetation. Rich, strong contrasts (orange-red and green, blue and orange) and shimmering, dappled light evoke the relaxed atmosphere of a bright summer's day. The pleasurable feeling is not disturbed by the unsightly litter or picnic remains that people often complained about at the time. Again, Renoir is following in the classical traditions of painting as in Puvis de Chavannes' allegory *The Promised Land*, but while the latter presents a scene from history, in Renoir's case, it seems as though Utopia may be found in the present.

Dancing Couples – Images of Vitality and Joy

The dream of everlasting, timeless, naturally-contented existence, hinted at in so many of Renoir's works, is developed further in his depictions of couples dancing made in 1882 and 1883.

In the evenings, the tables on the terrace of the Restaurant Fournaise were pushed to one side and, with a pianist to provide the music, there was dancing. Aline "danced the waltz divinely": in *Dance in the Country* (page 104) Renoir portrays her dancing in Lhote's arms on the terrace of the Restaurant Fournaise. Lhote is also the dancing partner for Marie-Clementine Valadon (who herself would become known as a painter under the pseudonym Suzanne Valadon) in *Dance in the City* (page 105): "My wife posed for one of the figures. The other woman was a model, Suzanne Valadon, who later went in for painting herself. My friend Lauth [sic] posed for the two male figures."[53] It is a matter of debate as to whether Suzanne Valadon, only seventeen at the time, also modelled for the figure in *Dance in Bougival* (page 103).

The three paintings were not painted as a group, and *Dance in Bougival* is somewhat larger than the other two. Also their titles are not definitive and were often changed. *Dance in Bougival* was also known, among other things, as *Danse à la Campagne* and as *Danse à Chatou*. It seems that Renoir used a pen-and-ink version of this motif for his illustration for Paul Lhote's short story "Zélia," which then served as a study for the painting. The young woman in this painting wears a ring, but it is not clear what her relationship may be to the man in whose arms she is dancing. And there is also a question mark over the connection between the group in the left background and the couple in the foreground. Whereas the portrayal of the dancers' physicality is fully developed, the group of figures in the background seems very sketchy, with the result that there is a distinct break between the background and the foreground. This illustrates well the problems that arise from Renoir's efforts to capture a certain atmosphere and yet to concentrate at the same time on a particular section of the picture.

Dance in the Country,
1882/83, detail

The motif of a dancing couple first occurs in *Alfred Sisley and his Wife* (page 107) in 1868. Whereas in *Le Moulin de la Galette* the couples are integrated into the community of revellers as a whole, in the portrayals of dancers in 1882 and 1883 – as in the *Luncheon* – the forms receive greater emphasis and the figures are more individual. In their unforced naturalness and contented abandon these individuals convey the feeling of people untrammelled by everyday cares and in harmony with nature.

Couple Dancing,
1882/83

Right:
Dance at Bougival,
1882/83

Dance in the Country,
1882/83

Right:
Dance in the City,
1882/83

The countrified, somewhat awkward couple in *Dance in the Country* bears little resemblance to the smart, elegantly reserved couple in *Dance in the City*. Apart from the fact that one couple is outside under chestnut trees while the other is inside with a hot-house plant as their backdrop, the country couple does not shrink from close physical contact and animated movement: the man's hat has already fallen off and the woman openly shows her pleasure. The bunch of violets – standing for innocence and humble devotion – and the burnt-out cigarette symbolize as memento mori the transience of the things of this world. The city couple, on the other hand, maintains more of a distance and their emotions are largely hidden from the viewer.

Renoir's portrayals of couples dancing are images of vitality and of the joy of life: they should be seen in contrast to the dehumanization of society through industrialization and mass-culture. When people dance, they are released from everyday cares and their innate powers – erotic ones included – come to the fore again.

After painting these pictures of people dancing, Renoir ceased to draw on contemporary, urban themes or couples for his subject matter. He appears to have no longer been interested in the relationships between men and women. From now onwards he found the much-celebrated innocence of the Golden Age in the country and nowhere else, and after 1885 he spent an increasing amount of time in Essoyes in Champagne, and even moved there in 1888.

The question as to why Renoir turned to predominantly timeless themes after the eighties is often explained as a consequence of his journey to Italy in 1882 and of his work on drawing form. Talking to his son Jean, Renoir himself said that, after his journey to Italy, he wanted to concentrate on just a few issues that were central to painting. At this time, Renoir also loosened his contacts to his bohemian friends in Paris and devoted himself more intensively to his partner Aline Charigot.

This, however, does not fully explain why he stopped painting scenes from urban life. In fact – even apart from the crisis of Impressionism itself – a crucial factor in this matter was the crisis in the art market. Following the Paris stock market crash of 1882, the French market for Impressionist paintings collapsed. The

Alfred Sisley and his Wife, 1868

dealer Paul Durand-Ruel had relied on this market and new collectors in the United States had yet to be won over. At the same time, Renoir's retreat into his own private life and his concentration on the individual were also reactions to the increasing demise of the individual in society which he saw as a direct consequence of industrialization. Jean Renoir repeatedly reports that his father expressed sentiments of this kind. His fears for the loss of individual identity were in marked contrast to his early works in which the sense of collective harmony derives specifically from all the people being together.

In keeping with Renoir's dream of a classless society, women were given a leading role in his work and this view became even stronger as the artist grew older. He felt that "the feminine" was bound up with "natural life" and represented the way back to the secret of our origins. And he felt that men, too, should participate in this "natural" order of instinct, emotions, and intuition.

After the 1880s, Renoir gradually transferred the realms of harmonious existence, which he had once set in Paris and its surroundings, into the freedom of nature, unbound by time or place. His preferred motifs were large-scale nudes with an aura of mythology and classical art. It seems that they held for him promise of the key to the paradise of the gods, which is what his painting was about: "The earth was the paradise of the gods ... that is what I want to paint."[54]

Three Women Bathing,
1883 – 85

Bathers in the Forest, ca. 1897

Pierre-Auguste Renoir (1841–1919)

Biographical Notes

1841
Pierre-Auguste Renoir is born in Limoges, the sixth child of Léonard and Marguerite (née Merlet). The familiy name is wirtten as Renouard.

1845
The Renouard family moves to Paris.

1849
Birth of Renoir's brother Edmond.

1854 – 58
Apprenticeship as a porcelain painter (paints flowers, later also portraits, on plates and vases); at the same time attends drawing courses at L'Ecole Gratuite de Dessin run by Callouette.

1858 – 59
Invention of printed designs for porcelain leads to Renoir painting fans, heraldic designs (for his brother Henri, who is an engraver), and, once he has completed his apprenticeship, also blinds for shops. Earns very well because he works so fast and skilfully.

1860
Makes first copies of paintings in the Louvre by Peter Paul Rubens, Jean-Honoré Fragonard, François Boucher.

1861
Attends the independent studio of the academic painter Charles Gleyre where he becomes acquainted with Frédéric Bazille, Claude Monet, and Alfred Sisley.

1862
Paints in the Forest of Fontainebleau with Monet. Meets Narcisse Diaz. Three months' military service.

1863
Drawing course at Ecole des Beaux-Arts. Becomes acquainted with Camille Pissarro and Paul Cézanne.

1864
Decides to become a professional artist. First painting accepted by the Salon (*La Esmeralda*).

1865
Two paintings accepted by the Salon (*Portrait of William Sisley* and *Soirée d'été*). Friendship with Jules Le Coeur whom he visits in Marlotte where he meets Lise Tréhot (his mistress and model until 1872). Becomes acquainted with Gustave Courbet.

1866
Paints with Sisley and Le Coeur in the Forest of Fontainebleau (*Cabaret of Mother Antony*).

1867
Shares a studio (until 1870) with Frédéric Bazille (*Frédéric Bazille at his easel*) in Rue dela Paix aux Batignolles. Paints in Chantilly. His painting, *Diana,* is rejected by the Salon.

Renoir's hand-painted porcelain vase, 1857, private collection

111

1868

Successful showing of *Lise* in the Salon. Suffers extreme financial privation. Stays at Ville d'Avray. Paints *Alfred Sisley and his wife*. First views of Paris (including *Skaters in the Bois de Bologne* and *Le Pont des Arts*)

1869

Exhibits in the Salon. Stays for the summer with his parents in Voisins-Louveciennes. Together with Monet paints different versions of *La Grenouillère*.

1870

Two paintings accepted by the Salon (including *Bather with a Griffon*). Called up for military service in the Franco-Prussian War; discharged due to ill-health.

Right: Renoir, ca. 1875

Below: Renoir, aged 19

1871

Convalescence in Bordeaux. Returns to Paris, studio in rue Notre-Dame-des-Champs. Stays in Marlotte.

1872

First picture sales (including *Le Pont des Arts*) to the art dealer (and supporter of Impressionism) Paul Durand-Ruel.

1873

Through Edgar Degas, meets the art critic and collector Théodore Duret who arranges sales of his works. Shows two works in the Salon des Refusés. Paints with Monet in Argenteuil (*Monet painting in his Garden at Argenteuil*). Studio (until 1883) at 35 rue Saint-Georges, which becomes a meeting place for many artists. Founding member (December 27) of the group of Impressionists (Société Anonyme Coopérative des Artistes Peintres, Sculpteurs, Graveurs). Falls out with the Le Coeur family.

1874

Participates in the first exhibition of what is to become known as Impressionism in the rooms of the photographer Nadar in Boulevard des Capucines. (The term "Impressionists" stems from a derogatory review by the critic Louis Leroy in the journal *Charivari*).
With Monet in Argenteuil in the summer (*The Seine at Argenteuil*), Manet and Sisley are also painting

Self-portrait,
ca. 1876

there. Becomes acquainted with the painter Gustave Caillebotte. Frequents Le Cafe de la Nouvelle – Athènes. Paints *The Theatre Box* (known as *La Loge*).

1875
Rents a studio at 12 rue Cortot near Le Moulin de la Galette. Paints *Nude in the Sunlight* (also known as *Torso d'Anna*). Together with Monet and Sisley organizes a sale of Impressionist works in the Hôtel Drouot, but with little success.
Paints the owners of the Restaurant Fournaise on the Ile de Chatou (*Alphonse Fournaise* and Alphonsine

Fournaise). Meets the collector Victor Chocquet (*Portrait of Victor Cocquet*).

1876
Shows 15 paintings in the second Impressionist exhibition. Paints in the garden in rue Cortot (*Garden in rue Cortot; The Swing*) and at Le Moulin de la Galette (*Le Moulin de la Galette*). Stays in Champrosay with the writer Alphonse Daudet.
Portraits of the publishing family Charpentier (*Madame Charpentier and her children*) and decorations for their house in rue de Grenelle.

Renoir, ca. 1885

1877

With Renoir's encouragement Georges Rivière publishes the journal *L'Impressionisme* (4 issues). Participates in the third Impressionist exhibition. Auction of Impressionist works in the Hôtel Drouot. Regularly attends the Wednesday meetings of artists at Eugène Murer's restaurant at 95 boulevard Voltaire.

1878

At the Café is accepted by the Salon. Illustrations for Emile Zola (*Au Bonheur des Dames*).

1879

Illustrations for Charpentier's newly founded journal *La vie moderne* (editor in chief is Renoir's brother Edmond). First solo exhibition in the journal's gallery space.
Declines to participate in the fourth Impressionist exhibition; instead shows four paintings in the Salon (including *Portrait of Jeanne Samary*). Stays with the Berard family in Wargemont and with Jacques-Emile Blanche in Dieppe, paints wall-decorations (on the theme of Richard Wagner) for Blanche's house.

1880

Does not take part in the fifth Impressionist exhibition. Shows four paintings in the Salon. Stays in Wargemont (*Geraniums*). Numerous commissions for portraits, among others for the financier Cahen d'Anvers (*Irène Cahen d'Anvers*).
Paints *Luncheon of the Boating Party* in the Restaurant Fournaise on Ile de Chatou.
Either during that summer or autumn meets his wife-to-be, Aline Charigot (1859–1915).

1881

Regular purchases by Durand-Ruel improve Renoir's financial situation and allow him to travel abroad for the first time.
March–April: trip to Algeria. Rents a studio on his return in rue Norvins.
Paints in Chatou; becomes acquainted with James Whistler. Does not participate in the sixth Impressionist exhibition; shows to works in the Salon. Stays in Wargemont.
October–December: trip to Italy (Venice, Padua, Florence, Rome, Naples, Calabria); Aline accompanies him on the last stage of the journey.

1882

January: returns to France; paints with Paul Cézanne in l'Estaque. Contracts pneumonia. Convalesces in Algeria.
Exhibits one portrait in the Salon.
Stays in Pourville and Dieppe where he meets Monet and J. E. Blanche.
Crash of the Paris stock market creates a crisis in the art market.

1883

Exhibits in the Salon. Solo exhibition in the Galerie Durand-Ruel.
Visits Caillebotte in Petit-Gennevilliers.
September: trip to Jersey.
Paintings of dances (*Dance in Bougival; Dance in the Country; Dance in the City*).
December: paints with Monet on the Mediterranean coast. Loosens ties with Impressionism and works on a new style of painting (his so-called "dry period").

1884

Works in the staticless painterly style of Ingres until about 1887 (*Children's afternoon at Wargemont*). Attends the monthly Impressionist dinners in Café Riche.

1885

Birth of his son Pierre (Caillebotte is godfather).
Paints with Cézanne in La Roche-Guyon near Giverny.
First stay in autumn in Essoyes, Aline's hometown.

114

Café Nouvelle Athènes in Mont-martre, a favorite meeting-place for artists, photograph 1906

Parisian street-scene, ca. 1890

Paints *The Bather*.
Suffers from depression.
During 1885 – 86 takes part in the gatherings at Berthe Morisot's.

1886
Eighth and last Impressionist exhibition held with-out the participation of Renoir, Monet, and Sisley.
Shows *The Bathers* in the Galerie Georges Petit.
Durand-Ruel objects to Renoir's new style.
Summer in La Roche-Guyon and in Brittany with Aline and Pierre.

View of rue Cortot in Montmartre where Renoir had a studio

1887
Becomes acquainted with the symbolist poet Stéphane Mallarmé.
Exhibits five works in Georges Petit's sixth Exposition Internationale.
Finishes *The Large Bathers* (begun in 1884).

1888
Visits Cézanne at his family's estate Le Jas de Bouffan in Aix-en-Provence. Durand-Ruel exhibits fifteen of his paintings.
Spends his time in Argenteuil, Essoyes, and Petit-Gennevilliers.
Rheumatism an slight paralysis of half of his face as a result of a persistent cold.

115

Above: Les Collettes, Renoir´s studio,
which now houses Cagnes Musuem,
photograph 1960

Left:
Mme. Renoir with Coco and Pierre, 1901/02

Below:
Studio in rue Saint-Georges,
1876/77

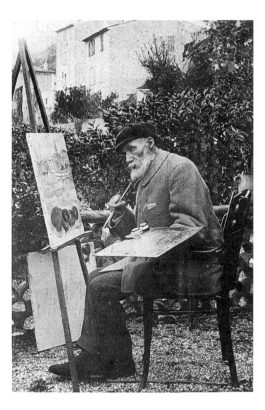

Renoir at his easel in front of the post office in Cagnes, 1903

collector Paul Gallimard; admires Velázquez and Goya in the Prado. Stays in Brittany (in Pont-Aven among other places). Paints the *Portrait of Stéphane Mallarmé*.

1893
Visits Beaulieu (Nice), Deauville, Essoyes, Pont-Aven. Jeanne Baudot becomes his pupil.

1894
Birth of his son Jean. Gabrielle Renard, Aline's cousin, becomes the children's nanny and a favourite model for Renoir. She stays until 1914. Becomes acquainted with the art-dealer Ambroise Vollard. Death of Caillebotte. Renoir offers Caillebotte's artistic estate to galleries in Paris, initially without success. Gout forces Renoir to use two walking-sticks.

1889
In Aix with Cézanne again. Relinquishes his strict style and returns to a more accessible style. Moves to 13 rue Girardon in Montmartre. Must take care to keep warm. Depression and doubts about his own painting.

1890
April 14: Renoir marries Aline Charigot, with whom he already has a son ("Château des Brouillards" in rue Girardon).

1891
Solo-exhibition put on by Durand-Ruel. Visits Caillebotte in Petit-Gennevilliers. Trip to the Midi (Tamaris-sur-Mer, Le Lavandou, Toulon, Nimes). Visits Berthe Morisot in Mézy.

1892
Successful exhibition with 110 works put on by Durand-Ruel brings him a greater degree of financial security. Trip to Spain (Madrid, Seville) with the

Self-portrait with White Hat, 1910

Renoir
in his studio,
Les Collettes,
1912

1895
In view of his health Renoir prefers the warm climate of Provence; paints in Martigues with his pupil Jeanne Baudot (*Portrait of Jeanne Baudot*). Visits Brittany and Normandy (with J. E. Blanche in Dieppe). Buys a house in Essoyes.
Falls out with Cézanne.

1896
Exhibition with 42 works in the Galerie Durand-Ruel. Trip to Germany (Dresden, Wagner Festival in Bayreuth). Studio in rue de la Rochefoucauld in Paris.

1897
Caillebotte's Impressionist collection donated to le Musée Luxembourg, Paris.

1898
First visit to Cagnes-sur-Mer. Summer in Essoyes.
Trip to Holland (Den Haag, Amsterdam). Impressed
by Vermeer.

1899
Spends time in the south of France because of
severe rheumatism (Cagnes, Grasse, thermal
treatment in Aix-les-Bains).
Exhibition (42 works) at the Galerie Durand-Ruel
together with Monet, Pissarro, and Sisley.
Auction of the Chocquet collection which includes
numerous works by Renoir including a replica of
the *Le Moulin de la Galette*).

1900
Exhibition in the Galerie Bernheim-Jeune of 68
works. Trip to the Midi. Shows 10 works in the Paris
World's Fair.
Made a Knight of the Legion of Honour. Progressive
rheumatism leads to deformation of his hands and
arms.

Renoir with Aline and Coco, *c.* 1912

Renoir in his studio, 1912

1901
Birth of his son Coco. Exhibition with 23 works at
Paul Cassirer's gallery in Berlin.
Flat and studio in Paris, rue Caulaincourt.

1902
In Cannet (Villa Printemps).
Exhibition with 40 works in the Galerie Durand-Ruel.
Serious deterioration of his health (rheumatism and
paralysis around his left eye).

1903
Due to illness, spends winters from now on in the
south of France (Le Cannet, Cagnes) and summers
in Paris and Essoyes.

1904
Ineffectual health treatments in Bourbonne-les-Bains.
Successful showing of 35 works in the autumn Salon
in Paris gives him new heart. Paints despite severe
pain.

1905
Winter in Cagnes, summer in Essoyes (new studio
there). Durand-Ruel shows 59 works in London.
Honorary president of the autumn Salon.

1906
Maurice Denis visits him in Cagnes. Meets Monet in
Paris.

1907
The Metropolitan Museum, New York, buys *Madame
Charpentier and her Children*. In Cagnes, acquires the
property Les Collettes (moves in in 1908).

Renoir´s apartment, boulevard de Clichy, Paris, 1915

1908
Visit by Aristide Maillol, subsequent experiments of his own with sculpture. Paints the *Portrait of Ambroise Vollard* and the mythological scene *The Judgement of Paris*. Exhibition put on by Durand-Ruel in New York. Monet visits him in Cagnes.

1909
Admires Monet's Water lilies in the Galerie Durand-Ruel. Paints despite physical pain (*The Clown*).

1910
Summer visit to Germany (Upper Bavaria). *Portrait of Paul Durand-Ruel*.

1911
Julius Meier-Graefe publishes a monograph on Renoir. Studio in the boulevard Rochechouart in Paris. Visits the south of France.

1912
January–March: severe rheumatism prevents him from working in the studio at Les Collettes. Visits Nice.
Exhibitions in the Galerie Thannhauser in Munich (41 works), put on by Durand-Ruel in New York (24 works), and in Paris (58 portraits).
June: severe paralysis confines Renoir to a wheelchair. Depression since he must stop painting for a while. Operation in Melon und convalescence in Chaville. Visits the south of France.
Paints many female nudes. His pictures fetch high prices.

1913
The Armory-Show in New York includes five works by Renoir.
Exhibitions in Paris put on by Bernheim-Jeune (52 works) and Manzi Joyant (30 works).

Richard Guino (a pupil of Maillol's) makes sculptures according to Renoir's desings (*Venus Victorious*, 1914, Tate Gallery, London).
Spends time at Les Collettes and Nice.

1914
Visit from Auguste Rodin and Jacques-Emile Blanche. Paints the portrait of the actress *Tilla Durieux*.

1915
Two of his sons are injured in the war. Aline dies.

1916
Divides his time between Paris and Cagnes.

1917
Exhibition of 18 works put on by Durand-Ruel in New York. Henri Matisse visits him in Cagnes.

1918
The Musée Luxembourg buys Renoir's *Portrait of Colonna Romano*.

Deterioration of his health. Suspected gangrene in his legs.

1919
Completes another painting entitled *The Large Bathers*. Becomes a Commander of the Legion of Honour. Exhibtion of 35 works at the Durand-Ruel gallery in New York.
Albert André publishes his monograph on Renoir. The Louvre buys Renoir's *Portrait of Madame Charpentier*.
Renoir dies of pneumonia in Cagnes on December 3.

Renoir, ca. 1916
Photograph: Archives Durand-Ruel

Renoir and his model, Andrée Heuschling, who later married his son Jean, ca. 1915

Right: The garden, Les Collettes

121

Notes

1 Prince Georges Bibesco, (1834–1902) was a friend of Frédéric Bazille who introduced him into the circle of Impressionists and to Renoir.

2 See also Georges Poisson, *Evocation du Grand Paris*, Paris 1960.

3 M. Catinat, *Les bords de la Seine avec Renoir et Maupassant*, Chatou 1952.

4 J.P. Palewski, "Les Impressionistes à Louveciennes", in: *Le Vieux Paris* 1963.

5 C. Monet in: Daniel Wildenstein, *Claude Monet, Catalogue raisonné* I, no. 53. See also letter from Renoir to Frédéric Bazille (1869) in: *Bazille et ses Amis*, Paris 1932, pp. 155–156.

6 Trans. from *L'Evénement illustré*, 20. 6. 1868.

7 Joel Isaacson, "Impressionism and Journalistic Illustration", in: *Arts Magazine*, June1982.

8 Contrary to what is often said, the colour black was used in numerous early Impressionist paintings, although Monet did avoid it after 1870 and Renoir did his best to replace black with a mixture of red and blue, that is to say, cobalt blue or ultramarine. In the end, however, he did come back to black, for in his view black was the "queen of colours". Ambroise Vollard, *Renoir: An Intimate Record*, trans. Harold L. Van Doren and Randolph Weaver, New York (1925) 1990, p. 52.

9 A semi-circular form (out of wire, whale-bone, or horse hair) worn underneath the skirt at the back and attached with ties at the waist.

10 Ambroise Vollard, *Renoir: An Intimate Record*, p. 17.

11 M. Wilson, "Monet's Bathers at la Grenouillère", in: *National Gallery, Technical Bulletin* 5: 1981, p. 23.

12 Transl. from Albert André, *Renoir*, Paris 1928, p. 30.

13 Ambroise Vollard, *Renoir: An Intimate Record*, p. 6.

14 Jean Renoir, *Renoir, My Father*, pp. 90–91.

15 See Edmond Duranty, *La Nouvelle Peinture*, new edition: Paris 1988, p. 23.

16 Ambroise Vollard, *Renoir: An Intimate Record*, p. 17.

17 Jean Hugueney, "Napoleon III et Haussmann", in: *Les monuments historiques de France* 20: 1974(1), pp. 20-27.

18 Jean Renoir, *Renoir, My Father*, p. 45.

19 Transl. from Gerard de Nerval *Promenades et souvenirs*, Paris 1852, as quoted in exh. cat. *Paris Belle Epoque*, Essen 1994, p. 71.

20 Lydia Maillard, *Les Moulins de Montmartre*, Paris 1981.

21 Pere Debray, himself a passionate amateur dancer, had an unusual repertoire of leaps and jumps which he used to teach the young people from the neighbourhood on Sundays, and it was this passion for dancing which gave him the idea of opening his own dance-hall.

22 Georges Rivière, *Renoir et ses Amis*, Paris 1921. Georges Rivière, an ardent defender of Impressionism, was a close friend of Renoir's and a frequent visitor in his studios in rue Saint-Georges and rue Cortot.

23 Wolfgang Schivelbusch, *Lichtblicke: Zur Geschichte der Künstlichen Helligkeit im 19. Jahrhundert*, Munich 1983, p. 45. Schivelbusch shows how the new concept of lighting, the preference for bright dispersed light, made an impact not only on the lighting in towns and homes but also on open-air painting.

24 "Der befreite Körper" ['The Freed Body'], in: Philippe Ariès and Georges Duby, *Geschichte des Privaten Lebens*, vol. 4: Von der Revolution zum Großen Krieg, Frankfurt/M 1992.

25 Jean Renoir, *Renoir, My Father*, p. 161.

26 Ambroise Vollard, *Renoir: An Intimate Record*, p. 28.

27 See exh. cat. *Renoir*, Paris 1985, p. 146.

28 Joel Isaacson, "Impressionism and Journalistic Illustration", in: *Arts Magazine*, June 1982.

29 Jean Renoir, *Renoir, My Father*, p. 82.

30 Barbara White, "Renoir's Sensous Women", in: *Woman as Sex Objects*, London 1973, pp. 167-181.

31 Edmond Renoir, "Cinquième exposition de la 'Vie moderne'", in: *La vie moderne*, 19.6.1876; reprinted in Lionello Venturi, *Les Archives des Impressionistes*, vol. 2, New York 1968, p. 337.

32 Jean Renoir, *Renoir, My Father*, p. 79.

33 Philippe Arriès and Georges Duby, *Geschichte des Privaten Lebens*, vol. 4: Von der Revolution zum Großen Krieg, Frankfurt/M 1992, p. 544 f.

34 *Das Tagebuch der Julie Manet*, Munich/Hamburg 1988, p. 150.

35 Jean Renoir, *Renoir, My Father*, p. 179.

36 François Gauzi, *Lautrec et son temps*, Paris 1954. Quoted in:

exh. cat. *Paris Belle Epoque*, Essen 1994, p. 85.

37 Paul Lhote, "Mademoiselle Zélia", in: *La vie moderne*, 3. 11. 1883.

38 Trans. from Jean Renoir, *Mein Vater Auguste Renoir*. Zürich 1981, p. 90.

39 See Julien Lemer, *Paris au Gaz*, Paris 1862, p. 15.

40 Transl. from Julius Rodenberg, *Paris bei Sonnenschein und Lampenlicht*, Leipzig 1867, p. 45, quoted in Wolfgang Schivelbusch, op. cit., p. 147.

41 Up until the beginning of the nineteenth century, it was usual for clothing that had been worn by the aristocracy to be passed on to the middle and lower classes by clothes dealers known as *marchandes à la toilette*.

42 The setting for Zola's "The Ladies' Paradise" (1883) is a large Paris department store in which the women fall victim to their own passion for shopping.

43 Jean Renoir, *Renoir, My Father,* p. 69.

44 Contemporary fashion plates were indubitably of interest to Renoir. This can be seen, among other examples, in his pastels for the journal *La Vie Moderne*, a weekly devoted to the latest in fashion, art, and culture that was founded in 1879 by Georges Charpentier and edited by Renoir's brother Edmont. Further evidence of his interest in fashion can be seen in his illustrations for Emile Zola's *Au Bonheur des Dames*. Cf. John Rewald, "Auguste Renoir and his brother",in: *Gazette de Beaux-Arts*, no. 87, 1945, p. 184.

45 Ambroise Vollard, *Renoir: An Intimate Record*, p. 69.

46 Jean Renoir, *Renoir, My Father,* p. 82.

47 Ambroise Vollard, *Renoir: An Intimate Record*, p. 56.

48 Ibid., p. 56.

49 Transl. from Emile Zola, "Der Salon von 1880", in: *Schriften zur Kunst*, Frankfurt 1988, pp. 247 and 231.

50 Ambroise Vollard, *Renoir: An Intimate Record*, p. 19.

51 For an identification of the figures, see the original French edition of Jean Renoir, *Renoir, My Father* (Renoir, Paris 1962), although this only offers one of several possible interpretations.

52 Transl. from Gaston Bachelard, *L´Eau et les Rêves*, Paris 1942.

53 Ambroise Vollard, *Renoir: An Intimate Record*, p. 33.

54 Transl. from Joachim Gasquet, "Le Paradis de Renoir", in: *Amour de l'art*, February 1921, s.p.

Selected Bibliography

As yet there is no wholly reliable catalogue of Renoir's work. Picture titles and dates vary or are unclear. Further problems are created by numerous forgeries which Renoir himself already complained about. (François Daulte's *Auguste Renoir: Catalogue Raisonné de l'Œuvre Peint*, vol. I, Lausanne 1971 has its limitations too).

Even contemporary sources are not always properly researched, and Renoir's own statements can be contradictory.

In addition to this, there was a long period when Renoir's work was neglected by art historians. The first critical and more comprehensive review of his work since 1933 was the large Renoir retrospective in 1985 in Paris, London, and Boston. Since the 1995/1996 exhibition in Tübingen, Renoir has become more prominent again in the public eye.

Georges Rivière, *Renoir et ses Amis*. Paris 1921.

Jeanne Baudot, *Renoir, ses Amis, ses Modèles*. Paris 1949.

Sophie Monneret, *Dictionnaire de l'Impressionisme et de son Epoque*. Paris 1978–1980.

Jean Renoir, *My Father Auguste Renoir*. Trans. Randolph T. and Dorothy Weaver, London 1962.

Barbara E. White, *Renoir: His Life, Art and Letters*. New York 1984.

Exh. cat. *Renoir*. Paris, Grand Palais/London, Hayward Gallery/Boston, Museum of Fine Arts 1985.

Julius Meier-Graefe, *Renoir*. Frankfurt/M. 1986 (First edition: Paris 1912).

Robert L. Herbert, *Impressionism: Art, Leisure and the Parisian Society*. New Haven and Lonon 1988.

André Albert and Marc Elder, *Renoir's Atelier*. San Francisco 1989 (First edition: Paris 1931).

Ambroise Vollard, *Renoir's Paintings, Pastels and Drawings*. San Francisco 1989 (First edition: Paris 1918/1919).

Sophie Monneret, *Renoir*, Cologne 1990.

Ambroise Vollard, *Renoir: An Intimate Record*. Trans. Harold L. Van Doren and Randolph T. Weaver, New York 1990 (First edition: 1925).

Derek Fell, *Renoirs Garden*. New York 1992.

Götz Adriani, *Renoir*. Cologne 1996.

Photo Credits

National Gallery of Art, Washington, ca. 1996, Board of Trustees: pages 92, 94

The National Gallery, London, Courtesy of the Trustees: pages 96, 97

Nationalmuseum, SKM, Stockholm: pages 6, 17, 19

Anneli Nau, Munich: plan on page 8

Philadelphia Museum of Art: pages 24, 39

Photographie Giraudon, Paris: front cover, pages 40, 51, 53, 58, 70, 100, 104, 105

Oskar Reinhart Collection "Am Römerholz", Winterthur: pages 12, 13

List of Illustrations

Dance at Bougival 1882/83
Oil on canvas,
71 ⅝ x 38 ⅝ in. (182 x 98 cm)
Museum of Fine Arts, Boston
Frontispiece, page 103

On a River Bank 1878 – 80
Oil on canvas,
29 ½ x 25 ⅞ in. (54.6 x 65.7 cm)
Private collection, USA
Page 4

La Grenouillère 1869
Oil on canvas,
26 x 33 ⅞ in. (66 x 86 cm)
Nationalmuseum, Stockholm
Pages 6, 17, 19

Jules Pelocq
La Grenouillère 1868
Engraving
Bibliothèque Nationale, Paris
Page 9, top

Edouard Riou
La Grenouillère à Bougival
Engraving for the magazine
La Chronique illustrée, 1.8.1869
Page 9, bottom

Ferdinand Heilbuth
La Grenouillère 1870
Oil on canvas
Private collection
Page 10

Bridge Near Paris 1875
Oil on canvas,
20 x 25 ⅝ in. (51 x 65.2 cm)
Sterling and Francine Clark Art
Institute, Williamstown, Mass.
Page 11

La Grenouillère 1869
Oil on canvas,
25 ⅝ x 36 ¼ in. (65 x 92 cm)
Collection Oskar Reinhart
"Am Römerholz," Winterthur
Pages 12/13

La Grenouillère 1869
Oil on canvas,
23 ¼ x 31 ½ in. (59 x 80 cm)
Puschkin Museum, Moscow
Page 15

Claude Monet
La Grenouillère 1869
Oil on canvas,
29 ⅛ x 39 ¼ in. (74 x 99.7 cm)
Metropolitan Museum of Art, New York
Page 16

Antoine Watteau
Embarkation for Cythera 1717
Oil on canvas,
50 ⅜ x 78 in. (128 x 198 cm)
Louvre, Paris
Page 20

Lise 1867
Oil on canvas,
71 ⅝ x 44 ½ in. (182 x 113 cm)
Folkwang Museum, Essen
Page 21

Diana 1867
Oil on canvas,
78 ½ x 51 in. (199.5 x 129.5 cm)
National Gallery, Washington
Page 23

Les grands Boulevards 1875
Oil on canvas,
20 ½ x 25 in. (52.1 x 63.5 cm)
Museum of Art, Philadelphia
Pages 24, 39

Leopold Lelée
Folies-Bergère —
Tous les Soirs Spectacle Varié
Colour lithograph,
48 ⅞ x 34 ⅝ in. (124 x 88 cm)
Deutsches Plakat Museum, Essen
Page 27

The Pont-Neuf, Paris 1872
Oil on canvas,
29 ½ x 37 in. (75 x 94 in.)
National Gallery, Washington
Pages 28/29

Pont des Arts, Paris 1867
Oil on canvas,
24 x 39 ⅜ in. (61 x 100 cm)
The Norton Simon Foundation,
Los Angeles
Page 31

Parisienne 1874
Oil on canvas,
63 x 41 ¾ in. (160 x 106 cm)
National Museum of Wales, Cardiff
Page 33

Narcisse Diaz de la Peña
The Forest near Fontainebleau
1874
Oil on panel,
15 ½ x 22 ½ in. (39.5 x 57.5 cm)
Musée des Beaux-Arts, Reims
Gift of J. Wannier-David
Photo: C. Devleeschauwer

Claude Monet
Le Déjeuner sur l'Herbe 1865/66
Central panel, oil on canvas,
97 ⅝ x 85 ⅜ in. (248 x 217 cm)
Musée d'Orsay, Paris
Page 35

The Cabaret of Mother Anthony
1866
Oil on canvas,
75 ⅝ x 50 ¾ in. (192 x 129 cm)
Nationalmuseum, Stockholm
Page 37

Claude Monet
Boulevard des Capucines 1873/74
Oil on canvas,
24 x 31 ½ in. (61 x 80 cm)
The Nelson-Atkins Museum of Art,
Kansas City
Page 38

Le Moulin de la Galette 1876
Oil on canvas,
51 ⅝ x 68 ⅞ in. (131 x 175 cm)
Musée d'Orsay, Paris
Pages 40, 51, 53

Jugglers at the Cirque Fernando
1879
Oil on canvas,
51 ⅛ x 38 ⅝ in. (130 x 98 cm)
Art Institute, Chicago
Page 43

*Portrait of Madame Charpentier
and her Children*   1878
Oil on canvas,
57 x 39 ⅜ in. (145 x 100 cm)
Metropolitan Museum of Art,
New York
Page 47

Le Moulin de la Galette   1876
Preliminary sketch
Oil on canvas,
25 ⅝ x 33 ½ in. (65 x 85 cm)
Ordrupgaardsamlingen, Copenhagen
Page 49

Le Moulin de la Galette   1876
Oil on canvas,
30 ¾ x 44 ½ in. (78 x 113 cm)
Formerly collection John Hay Whitney,
New York
Page 52

The Swing   1876
Oil on canvas,
36 ¼ x 28 ¾ in. (92 x 73 cm)
Musée d'Orsay, Paris
Page 55

The Arbour   1875
Oil on canvas,
38⅞ x 25 ⅝ in. (81 x 65 cm)
Puschkin Museum, Moscow
Page 56

Margot   1876/77
Oil on canvas,
18 ⅛ x 15 in. (46 x 38 cm)
Musée d'Orsay, Paris
Page 57

Nude in the Sunlight   1875/76
(Torso d'Anna)
Oil on canvas,
31 ⅞ x 25 ½ in. (81 x 64.8 cm)
Musée d'Orsay, Paris
Page 58

Garden in rue Cortot   1876
Oil on canvas,
59 ½ x 38 ½ in. (151 x 97 cm)
Carnegie Institute, Pittsburgh
Page 61

La Loge   1874
Oil on canvas,
31 ½ x 24 ¾ in. (80 x 63 cm)
Courtauld Institute, London
Page 62

Illustration for Zola's
Au bonheur des Dames   1883
Engraving
Private collection
Page 64

Edouard Manet
Parisienne: Dress with a Train
1875
Oil on canvas,
74 ¾ x 48 ½ in. (190 x 123 cm)
Nationalmuscm, Stockholm
Page 64, right

*Portrait of the Artist
Jeanne Samary*   1878
Oil on canvas,
68 ⅛ x 40 ½ in. (173 x 103 cm)
Hermitage, St. Petersburg
Page 65

Studying a Role   1874
Oil on panel,
Musée de St-Denis, Reims
Page 66

Jeanne Samary   1877
Oil on canvas,
22 x 18 ⅛ in. (56 x 46 cm)
Puschkin Museum, Moscow
Page 67

Madame Charpentier   1876/77
Oil on canvas,
18 ⅛ x 15 in. (46 x 38 cm)
Musée d'Orsay, Paris
Page 68, top

*Berthe Morisot and her
Daughter*   1894
Pastel,
23 ¼ x 17 ⅞ in. (59 x 45.5 cm)
Petit Palais, Paris
Page 68, bottom

Young Woman Braiding her Hair
1876
Oil on canvas,
22 x 18 ⅛ in. (56 x 46 cm)
National Gallery of Art, Washington
Page 69

Woman Reading   ca. 1876
Oil on canvas,
18 ⅛ x 15 in. (46 x 38 cm)
Musée d'Orsay, Paris
Page 70

Lady at the Piano   ca. 1875
Oil on canvas,
36 ⅝ x 29 ⅛ in. (93 x 74 cm)
Art Institute, Chicago
Page 72

*The Young Woman Reading an
Illustrated Journal*   1880/81
Oil on canvas,
18 ⅛ x 22 in. (46 x 56 cm)
Rhode Island Museum of Art
Page 73

After the Luncheon   1879
Oil on canvas,
39 ⅜ x 38 ⅞ in. (100 x 81 cm)
Städelsches Kunstinstitut,
Frankfurt a. M.
Page 74, top

Edgar Degas
Absinthe   1876
Oil on canvas,
37 x 27 ½ in. (94 x 70 cm)
Musée d'Orsay, Paris
Page 74, right

Edouard Manet
Chez le Père Lathuille   1879
Oil on canvas,
36 ⅝ x 44 ⅛ in. (93 x 112 cm)
Musée des Beaux-Arts, Tournai
Page 74, bottom

At the Café   ca. 1877/78
Oil on canvas,
11 ⅝ x 13 ⅝ in. (39.5 x 34.5 cm)
Private collection
Page 75

La Loge   ca. 1874
Oil on canvas,
10 ⅝ x 8 ⅝ in. (27 x 22 cm)
Collection Durand-Ruel, Paris
Page 76

La Première Sortie   1876
Oil on canvas,
25 ⅝ x 19 ⅝ in. (65 x 50 cm)
National Gallery, London
Page 77

Dancer 1874

Oil on canvas,
55 ⅞ x 37 in. (142 x 94 cm)
National Gallery, Washington
Page 79

*Luncheon of the Boating
Party* 1880/81

Oil on canvas,
51 ⅛ x 28 ¾ in. (130 x 73 cm)
Phillips Collection, Washington
Pages 80, 86/87, 89

On the Terrace 1881

Oil on canvas,
39 ⅜ x 31 ½ in. (100 x 80 cm)
Art Institute, Chicago
Page 83

Eugène Le Poutevin
Near Etretat 1865

Oil on canvas
Musée d'Art Moderne, Troyes
Page 84, top

The Boaters 1880/81

Pastel on paper,
Museum of Fine Arts, Boston
Bequest of Alvan T. Fuller
Page 91

Oarsmen in Chatou 1879

Oil on canvas,
31 ⅞ x 39 ⅜ in. (81 x 100 cm)
National Gallery of Art, Washington,
Gift of Sam A. Lewisohn
Pages 92, 94

The Rowing-Boat 1878 – 80

Oil on canvas,
21 ½ x 25 ¾ in. (54.5 x 65.5 cm)
Stiftung Langmatt, Sidney und Jenny
Brown, Baden, Switzerland
Page 95

Boats on the Seine 1879
(Seine at Asnières)

Oil on canvas,
28 x 36 ¼ in. (71 x 92 cm)
National Gallery, London
Pages 96/97

Gustave Caillebotte
Périssoires (Rowers) 1878

Oil on canvas,
61 x 42 ½ in. (155 x 108 cm)
Musée des Beaux-Arts, Rennes
Page 98, right

Frédéric Bazille
Summer Scene, Bathers 1869

Oil on canvas,
63 ⅜ x 63 ⅜ in. (161 x 161 cm)
Fogg Art Museum, Harvard University,
Cambridge, Mass.
Page 98, left

Return of a Boating Party 1862

Oil on canvas, 20 x 24 in. (50.8 x 61 cm)
Collection Cummings, Montreal
Page 99

Dance in the Country 1882/83

Oil on canvas,
70 ⅞ x 35 ⅜ in. (180 x 90 cm)
Musée d'Orsay, Paris
Pages 100, 104

Couple Dancing 1882/83

Ink on paper
Collection Henry P. McIlhenney,
Philadelphia
Page 102

Dance in the City 1882/83

Oil on canvas,
70 ⅞ x 35 ⅜ in. (180 x 90 cm)
Musée d'Orsay, Paris
Page 105

Alfred Sisley and his Wife 1868

Oil on canvas,
41 ⅜ x 29 ½ in. (105 x 62 cm)
Wallraf-Richartz Museum, Köln
Page 107

Three Women Bathing 1883 – 85

Pencil, 42 ½ x 24 ⅜ in. (108 x 62 cm)
Louvre, Cabinet des Dessins, Paris
Gift of Jacques Laroche
Page 108

Bathers in the Forest ca. 1897

Oil on canvas,
29 x 39 ¼ in. (73.7 x 99.7 cm)
The Barnes Foundation, Merion, Penn.
Page 109

Self-portrait ca. 1876

Oil on canvas,
11 ⅜ x 8 ⅞ in. (29 x 22.5 cm)
The Fogg Art Museum, Harvard
University, Cabridge, Mass.
Bequest of Maurice Wertheim
Page 113

*Studio in rue
Saint-Georges* 1876/77

Oil on canvas,
18 ⅛ x 15 in. (46 x 38 cm)
Norton Simon Foundation, Pasadena
Page 116

Self-portrait with White Hat 1910

Oil on canvas,
16½ x 13 in. (42 x 33 cm)
Private collection
Page 117

© Prestel-Verlag, Munich · New York, 1996

Front cover: *Le Moulin de la Galette*, 1876, detail; see p. 53
Spine and frontispiece: *Dance at Bougival*, 1882-83, detail; see p. 103
Page 4: *On a River Bank*, 1878

Translated from the German by Fiona Elliott
Edited by Jacqueline Guigui-Stolberg

Prestel-Verlag
Mandlstrasse 26 · D-80802 Munich, Germany
Tel.: (89) 381709-0; Fax: (89) 381709-35
and 16 West 22nd Street, New York, NY 10010, USA
Tel.: (212) 627-8199; Fax: (212) 627-9866

Prestel books are available worldwide.
Please contact your nearest bookseller or write to either
of the above addresses for information concerning
your local distributor.

Typeset by Reinhard Amann, Aichstetten
Lithography by Eurocrom 4, Villorba (TV)
Printed by Passavia Druckerei GmbH Passau
Bound by MIB Conzella, Aschheim
Typeface: Century Old Style

Printed on acid-free paper

Printed in Germany

ISBN 3-7913-1723-7 (English edition)
ISBN 3-7913-1712-1 (German edition)